The
Little
Big
Book
of
Dogs

The Little Big Book of Dogs

Edited by
ALICE WONG
and
LENA TABORI

Designed by
TIMOTHY SHANER
and
CHRISTOPHER MEASOM

welcome
BOOKS

NEW YORK · SAN FRANCISCO

Published in 2006 by Welcome Books®
An imprint of Welcome Enterprises, Inc.
6 West 18th Street, New York, NY 10011
(212) 989-3200; Fax (212) 989-3205
www.welcomebooks.com

Publisher: Lena Tabori
Project Director: Alice Wong
Designers: Timothy Shaner and Christopher Measom
Project Assistants: Jeffrey McCord and Maren Gregerson
Living with Dogs, Training and Behavior, Fun and Games,
and Doggy Treats text by Ellen Leach
Dogs of Distinction text by Jeffrey McCord
Line illustrations on pages 122, 123, and 346 by Kate DeWitt

Front jacket illustration by McClelland Barclay

Library of Congress Cataloging-in-Publication Data

Little big book of dogs / edited by Alice Wong and Lena Tabori.— 1st ed.
p. cm.
1. Dogs--MIscellanea. I. Wong, Alice. II. Tabori, Lena.
SF426.2.L58 2006
636'.7—dc22   2005035505

ISBN-10: 1-932183-90-6
ISBN-13: 978-1-932183-90-0

Printed in China

FIRST EDITION

1 3 5 7 9 10 8 6 4 2

Contents

The Thin Red Leash *James Thurber* 177
Crimes Against Dog *Alice Walker* 128
A Letter to the ASPCA *E. B. White* 209
Obituary *E. B. White* 348
Brownie *T. H. White* 323

Foreword 9

Stories & Essays

Dogs Vis-à-Vis Cats *Roy Blount, Jr.* 38
Fred, a Dog Gone But Not Forgotten
   Thomas M. Boyd 299
Every Dog Should Own a Man
   Corey Ford 25
Roy: From Rags to Riches
   James Herriot 114
A Woman's Best Friend *Erica Jong* 253
The Color of Joy *Caroline Knapp* 13
Lassie Come Home *Eric Knight* 184
The Love-Master: From White Fang
   Jack London 84
A Conversation with My Dogs
   Merrill Markoe 142
Blood Will Tell *Don Marquis* 238
A Dog's Life *Peter Mayle* 67
Stickeen *John Muir* 268
The Soul of a Dog *Daniel Pinkwater* 138
Sleeping with the Pack *Michael J. Rosen* . . 101
Travels with Charley *John Steinbeck* 158
The Dog Book *Albert Payson Terhune* . . . 219

Poetry

My Comforter *Anonymous* 51
The Hairy Dog *Herbert Asquith* 313
The Dollar Dog *John Ciardi* 247
Another Reason Why I Don't Keep
   a Gun in the House *Billy Collins* 134
#86 *Lawrence Ferlinghetti* 304
Power Source *Edward Field* 111
Let's Hit the Road *Maya Gottfried* 56
The Dog *Edgar A. Guest* 20
Poor Rover *Langston Hughes* 110
Confession of a Glutton *Don Marquis* . . . 338
To a Foolish Dog *Ogden Nash* 170
Ode to the Dog *Pablo Neruda* 200
Verses for a Certain Dog
   Dorothy Parker 124
Meditatio *Ezra Pound* 292
Man and Dog *Siegfried Sassoon* 94
Beautiful Joe *Marshall Saunders* 280
Birch *Karen Shepard* 77
But Mom Didn't Like Dogs
   Dr. Donald R. Stoltz 260
Dogs and Weather *Winifred Welles* 234

Contents

Living with Dogs

Adopting a Dog 16
Arrival Day Checklist 34
Bathtime! 314
Canine Culture 258
Dog Dietetics 101 334
Dog FAQs 290
The Dog Life Cycle 46
The Dog Park 172
Doggy Data 156
Dogspeak 136
Fido's Favorites: Tips for Using Treats 74
From Head to Tail: Grooming Your Dog . 308
Helping the Medicine Go Down 109
Pooch Playtime: Top Ten Dog Toys 64
Preserving the Novelty 216
Puppyproofing Your Home 168

Training & Behavior

Housebreaking Your New Arrival
    *Crate Training, Eliminate on
    Command, Pads, Paper* 78
Obsessive Activities *Speak! Hush!
    Getting a Motor-Mouth under
    Control, Digging and Scratching* 140
Party Manners *Jumping, Humping,
    and Other Obnoxious Behaviors* 344
Rules of the Run: Playing Nicely with
    Others *Fighting, Chasing* 204

Street Smarts: Stepping Out 174
Teaching the HEEL 294
Teaching the INSTANT RECALL 232
Teaching the SIT 264
Teaching TAKE IT and LEAVE IT 320
The Ten Worst Doggy Delinquencies 22
Toothy Etiquette: Chewing, Biting, and
    Fighting *Choosy Chewing, Soften
    the Bite: Appropriate Roughhousing* 112
Training 101 *Boot Camp for Dog Owners* . . 52

Dogs of Distinction

Bobbie the Wonder Dog 30
Chips the War Dog 180
Eve the Protector 123
Hachiko: True Loyalty 122
Kibbles 'n Bits Dog Heroes of the Year . . . 212
Owney the U.S. Mail Dog 58
Patches' Devotion 300
Presidential Dogs 152
Rin Tin Tin 276
Russian Space Dogs 318
Smokey the Mascot Soldier 98
Superhero Pit Bull 346
Tales That Wag the Dog 196
Tang the Guardian 248
The Well-Bred Dog 230

Contents

Canine Crackups

An Amazin' Mutt 72
Dog Haikus 256
Dog Rules 37
Dog Sayings... And What They Mean 198
Doggy Dictionary 106
Five Crucial Food Groups
    According to Dogs 342
He's a Very Smart Dog 72
How Many Dogs Does It Take
    to Change a Lightbulb? 164
New Year's Resolutions for Dogs 336
Things Dogs Must Remember 45
Things We Can Learn from a Dog 19
What Dog Loves to Take Bubble Baths? . . 288
What is a Dog's Artistic Medium? 306
When Good Dogs Go and Crossbreed 229
You Know You Are a Dog Person When... 132

Fun & Games

Activities for Groups *The Recall Game,*
    Doggy Circus, Birthday Party 155
Dog Agility 97
Dog Sports *Frisbee, Flyball Racing,*
    Dock Diving, Terrier Races 332
Fetch! 278
Playtime! *Hide-and-Seek-for-Treats,*
    Keepaway, Clean up Your Toys 62
Puppy Push-Ups 303
Search and Destroy 166

Doggy Treats

Cheesy Treats 340
Chewy Chicken Nuggets 33
Glazed Bones 126
Homemade Liver Snaps 251
Patty-Cake Appetizers 183
Peanut Butter Biscuits 317

My first dog was named *Bosse*, which means "little boy" in Swedish. I was three, and had just arrived in a America. He was brown, a standard poodle and ridiculously clever. I taught him to open doors. He could crawl across the floor like a soldier with a rifle. He could play dead for as long as I instructed him. He could balance an apple on his head. I loved him and he loved me. When I was in high school I loved again, and named her *Lady*, after *Lady and the Tramp*. She came from a shelter in Los Angeles. They told us she was part wolf, part shepherd, and part collie. She had extraordinary wisdom. She traveled by train with me from and to Montana, where she learned to herd cows, fell for a border collie, and came home to give birth to nine cowboy puppies. The dad, Joe, didn't even write. By the time she died I had children of my own, and we adopted another four-legged guru, Solo, from a shelter in Brooklyn. Part borzoi, part collie, she, too, had nine puppies after we met a golden on the street and discussed his qualifications. "Is he smart?" I

Foreword

asked. "Well," his owner said, "if you mean sit up and beg, no, but if you mean take a left around the corner, you've got your man." Of the nine puppies, we kept two until they died five years ago, two years after Solo, who I mourned for more than a year.

How I lived from then until last September without a dog, I can't say. I only knew I couldn't travel back and forth between San Francisco (where I spend half my time with my fiancé, Franco) and New York (where my main office and my daughters are) putting a dog in the hold each time. Finally, Franco said, "Couldn't the dog be small enough to travel under your seat?" And, so, for my birthday, came Maggie, a tiny silky mix. She's joyous. She's fearless. She's forgiving. She's generous. She's hilarious. And she's incredibly good. She's faster than a jackrabbit, chases every pinecone in sight, growls ferociously while playing tug of war but never forgets she is pretending, kisses my toes, and, greets me as if I have been gone forever, whether it is two minutes or two days.

These dogs explain my passion for dogs. Of course, this book is packed with other dogs, other stories and other people's love for them. Every story and poem, every idea, suggestion, and piece of advice in this book comes from love: intense, personal, intimate love between a person and a dog. Enjoy it curled up with your special pooch.

–Lena Tabori

I am I because my little dog knows me.

—GERTRUDE STEIN

The Color of Joy
by Caroline Knapp

Before you get a dog, you can't quite imagine what living with one might be like; afterward, you can't imagine living any other way. Life without Lucille? Unfathomable, to contemplate how quiet and still my home would be, and how much less laughter there'd be, and how much less tenderness, and how unanchored I'd feel without her presence, the simple constancy of it. I once heard a woman who'd lost her dog say that she felt as though a color were suddenly missing from her world: The dog had introduced to her field of vision some previously unavailable hue, and without the dog, that color was gone. That seemed to capture the experience of loving a dog with eminent simplicity. I'd amend it only slightly and say that if we are open to what they have to give us, dogs can introduce us to several colors, with names like *wildness* and *nurturance* and *trust* and *joy*.

Fall in love with a dog, and in many ways you enter a new orbit, a universe that features not just new colors but new rituals, new rules, a new way of experiencing attachment.

Everything shifts in this new orbit, sometimes subtly,

13

sometimes dramatically. Walks are slower: You find yourself
ambling up a city street instead of racing to a destination,
the dog stopping to sniff every third leaf, every other twig,
every bit of debris or detritus in your path. The clothes
are different: Predog, I used to be very finicky and self-
conscious about how I looked; now I schlep around in the
worst clothing—big heavy boots, baggy old sweaters, a
hooded down parka from L.L. Bean that makes me look like
an astronaut. The language is different, based on tone and
nuance instead of vocabulary. Even the equipment is new
and strange: You find yourself ordering unthinkable prod-
ucts from the Foster & Smith catalog (smoked pigs' ears,
chicken-flavored toothpaste), and you find your living-room
floor littered with sterilized beef bones and rawhide chips
and plastic chew toys and ropes and balls, and you find
your cupboards stocked with the oddest things—freeze-dried
liver cubes, tick shampoo, poop bags.

The internal shifts are bigger, sometimes life altering.
When you speak to people about what it's like to live with a
dog, you hear them talk about discovering a degree of solace
that's extremely difficult to achieve in relationships with
people, a way of experiencing solitude without the loneliness. You hear them talk about the dog's capacity to wrest

their focus off the past and future and plant
it firmly in the present, with the hear-and-
now immediacy of a romp on the living-
room rug or a walk in the woods. You
hear them talk about joys that are
exquisitely simple and pure: what it's
like to laugh at a dog who's doing something ridiculous, and how soothing it is to sit
and brush a dog's coat, and how gratifying it
is to make a breakthrough in training a dog,
to understand that you're communicat-
ing effectively with a different
species. Above all, you hear them
talk about feeling *accepted* in a new
way, accompanied through daily
life and over the course of
years by a creature who
bears witness to every
change, every shift in
mood, everything we do
and say and experience,
never judging us when
we falter or fail. 🐾

Adopting a Dog

Before you adopt, think seriously about whether you can afford the time and money required to care for an animal that can live up to 15 years, or even longer. People have been known to change their entire lifestyles, even their jobs, for their love of dogs. Dogs especially need a lot of physical companionship, and therefore require a deep emotional commitment as well as your time. Will this be your first dog, or are you already an established dog person? Are you away at work for extended periods? Will you carry the pooch with you or do you need a fenced yard? Will your dog be good with children? What about grooming? Can walking on a leash and playtime provide the exercise needed? As for nutrition, some breeds have requirements so specialized that they are not recommended for the general population. So before you fall in love with that dalmation's spots, know that this breed is so prone to kidney disease it requires a special low-protein diet and frequent checkups. Know your breed before you adopt.

If pedigree is not an issue, there are abandoned animals of all shapes and sizes waiting at your local rescue shelter for good homes. Just add love! Many organizations, including the American Society for the Protection of Animals (ASPCA), Humane Society, Bide-A-Wee, and local pet rescue groups will defray the cost of spaying and neutering as well as vaccinations, and provide low-cost top-notch health care in their veterinary clinics. Or you might consider obtaining a greyhound from the Greyhound Project, an international organization dedicated to educating the public about the plight of racing dogs. These gentle animals—wonderful around children and other dogs— will sneak into your heart and find a place to curl up.

If you are adopting a purebred, you can receive either papers or a certificate through an AKC-authorized breeder. Choose a reputable kennel with checkable references and a proven track record in addition to certification. Pet shops are not recommended as places to purchase puppies; if you do so, you may be supporting large, inhumane puppy mills that habitually truck these poor creatures across the United States in hot, crowded, unventilated vans. Most good breeders will not deal with pet stores, and will not allow a dog to go to a home they feel is unsuitable.

Things We Can Learn from a Dog

- Allow the experience of fresh air and the wind in your face to be pure ecstasy.

- When loved ones come home, greet with enthusiasm.

- Take naps and stretch before rising.

- Run, romp, and play daily.

- Be loyal.

- Never pretend to be something you're not.

- Don't go out without ID.

- Be aware of when to hold your tongue and when to use it.

- Leave room in your schedule for a good nap.

- If it's not wet and sloppy, it's not a real kiss.

- Avoid biting when a simple growl will do.

- On warm days, stop to lie on your back in the grass.

- When someone is having a bad day, be silent, sit close by, and nuzzle them gently.

- Delight in the simple joys of a long walk.

- If what you want lies buried, dig until you find it.

The Dog by Edgar A. Guest

I like a dog at my feet when I read,
Whatever his size or whatever his breed.
A dog now and then that will nuzzle my hand
As though I were the greatest of men in the land,
And trying to tell me it's pleasant to be
On such intimate terms with a fellow like me.

I like a dog at my side when I eat,
I like to give him a bit of my meat;
And though mother objects and insists it is bad
To let dogs in the dining room, still I am glad
To behold him stretched out on the floor by my chair.
It's cheering to see such a faithful friend there.

A dog leads a curious life at the best.
By the wag of his tail is his pleasure expressed.
He pays a high tribute to man when he stays
True to his friend to the end of his days.
And I wonder sometimes if it happens to be
That dogs pay no heed of the faults which men see.

Should I prove a failure; should I stoop to wrong;
Be weak at a time when I should have been strong,
Should I lose my money, the gossips would sneer
And fill with my blundering many an ear,
But still, as I opened my door, I should see
My dog wag his tail with a welcome for me.

The Ten Worst Doggy Delinquencies

1. Soiling the House Your dog communicates through pee-mail and poop-mail. Crate training is the way to prevent housebreaking issues (*page 78*).

2. Howling and Barking He's saying, Listen to meeeee! Train him to speak, and you can train him to hush (*page 140*).

3. Digging and Scratching Your bored canine has taken up yard work. Somebody, please, let the dog in! (*page 140*)

4. Chewing up things If your puppy's teeth are all over everything, don't let her near those shoes! (*pages 112*).

5. Biting and Mouthing Dogs bite—that's what they do. Help him learn bite moderation (*page 113*).

6. Jumping On/Humping Visitors His manners are atrocious. He's a dog! Teach him to sit when a guest enters the room (*page 344*).

7. Misbehaving on Leash She's a handful on urban streets. Teach your dog to heel, the gentle way (*page 294*).

8. Running Away or Failure to Come When Called Train a reliable recall (*page 232*). You can also play the Recall Game (*page 155*).

9. Fighting Your canine does not play nicely with others. Avoid being the terror of the neighborhood (*page 204*).

10. Chasing He takes off after cars, cyclists, joggers, cats—anything that moves. Modify his prey drive (*page 205*).

Every Dog Should Own a Man

by Corey Ford

Every dog should have a man of his own. There is
nothing like a well-behaved person around the house
to spread the dog's blanket for him, or bring him supper when he comes home man-tired at night.

For example, I happen to belong to an English setter who
acquired me when he was about six months old and has been
training me quite successfully ever since. He has taught me
to shake hands with him and fetch his ball. I've learned not
to tug at the leash when he takes me for a walk. I am completely housebroken, and I make him a devoted companion.

The first problem a dog faces is to pick out the right
man—a gay and affectionate disposition is more important
than an expensive pedigree. I do not happen to be registered
but my setter is just as fond of me as though I came from a
long line of blue bloods. Also, since a dog is judged by the
man he leads, is it a good idea to walk the man up and
down a couple of times to make sure his action is free and
he has springy hindquarters.

The next question is whether the dog and man should
share the house together. Some dogs prefer a kennel because

it is more sanitary, but my setter decided at the start that
he'd move right in the house with me. I can get into any
of the chairs I want except the big overstuffed chair in the
living room, which is his.

Training a man takes time. Some men are a little slow to
respond, but a dog who makes allowances and tries to put
himself in the man's place will be rewarded with a loyal
pal. Men are apt to be high-strung and sensitive, and a dog
who loses his temper will only break a man's spirit.

Punishment should be meted out sparingly—more can
be accomplished by a reproachful look than by flying off
the handle. My setter has never raised a paw to me, but
he has cured me almost entirely of the habit of running
away. When he sees me start to pick up my suitcase he
just lies down on the floor with his chin in his forepaws
and gazes at me sadly. Usually I wind up by canceling my
train reservations.

The first thing to teach a man is to stay at heel. For this
lesson the dog should hook one end of a leash to his collar
and loop the other end around the man's wrist to he cannot
get away. Start down the street slowly, pausing at each telephone pole until the man realizes that he's under control.
He may tug and yank at first, but this be discouraged
by slipping deftly between his legs and winding the leash
around his ankles. If the man tries to run ahead, brace all

four feet and halt suddenly, thus jerking him flat on his back. After a few such experiences the man will follow his dog with docility. Remember, however, that all such efforts at discipline must be treated as sport, and after a man has sprawled on the sidewalk the dog should lick his face to show him it was all in fun.

Every man should learn to retrieve a rubber ball. The way my setter taught me this trick was simple. He would lie in the center of the floor while I carried the ball on the far side of the room and rolled it toward him, uttering the word "Fetch!" He would watch the ball carefully as it rolled past him under the sofa. I would then get the ball from under the sofa and roll it past him again, giving the same command, "Fetch!"

This lesson would be repeated until the setter was asleep. After I got so I would retrieve the ball every time I said "Fetch!" my dog substituted other articles for me to pick up, such as an old marrow bone or a piece of paper he found in the wastebasket.

The matter of physical conditioning is important. A man whose carriage is faulty, and who slouches and droops his tail, is a reflection of the dog who owns him. The best way to get him in shape is to work him constantly and never give him a chance to relax. Racing him up and down the street at the end of a leash is a great conditioner. If he attempts to slump in the easy chair when he gets back, the dog should leap into it ahead of him and force him to sit in a straight-backed chair to improve his posture. And be sure to get him several times a night to go out for a walk, especially if it is raining.

Equally important is diet. Certain liquids such as beer have a tendency to bloat a man, and a dog should teach him restraint by jumping up at him and spilling his drink, or tactfully knocking the glass off the table with a sweep of his tail.

Not every dog who tries to bring up a man is as successful as my setter. The answer lies in understanding. The dog must be patient and not work himself up into a tantrum if his man can't learn to chase rabbits or wriggle under fences as well as a dog does. After all, as my setter says, it's hard to teach an old man new tricks.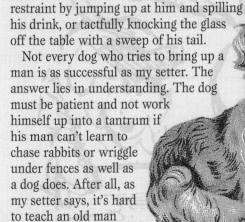

Bobbie the Wonder Dog

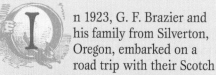

I n 1923, G. F. Brazier and his family from Silverton, Oregon, embarked on a road trip with their Scotch collie, Bobbie, in tow and discovered the incredible extent of their dog's loyalty. While the family stopped in Wolcott, Indiana, for a visit, several aggressive dogs confronted Bobbie, frightening him and chasing him away. The family scoured the town, honking their car's horn, to which he would habitually come running, and found nothing. They took out an ad in the local paper the next day to no avail, and remained in Wolcott for several more weeks. After an exhaustive search for their beloved pet, the brokenhearted family returned home to Oregon without Bobbie. Six months later, Bobbie returned to his hometown of Silverton, nearly 3,000 miles from where he vanished,. He had lost a significant amount of weight, and his paws were worn to the bone. Following the dog's celebrated return, many people sent letters to the Brazier family citing different stages of the dog's journey. According to various accounts, Bobbie would hop in a family's car and ride to their destination, or he would stop at a random house and quickly search for his old family, accepting food and care for his ailments only after he confirmed their absence. He would depart again before breakfast the following morning. Bobbie's detours with the families

who wished to adopt him added hundreds of miles onto his already grueling journey home. Witness accounts of his journey confirmed that Bobby braved crossing the Mississippi River, traveled through the Midwestern plains and the Western desert, and traversed many treacherous mountain ranges. In the end, he not only traveled the cross-country stretch on foot, but research and mapping of his course proved that he charted an incredibly logical and direct route. He arrived in Silverton, gaunt but spirited, trotting along the road, when he recognized Nova Brazier, one of the daughters of his family. Much to the astonishment and relief of his family, Bobbie jumped into their arms with obvious recognition and utter joy. He later savored his first meal at home—a sirloin steak and pint of cream—in the company of his family. 🐾

As dogs age, their teeth and gums become more sensitive, just like ours. These nuggets are great softer treats for an older dog or tasty training treats for all ages.

3 small jars chicken baby food*
1 tablespoon finely chopped parsley
1/4 cup powdered milk
1/4 cup wheat germ

1. Preheat oven to 350°F.

2. Combine all ingredients in a bowl and mix well. Roll into 1/2-teaspoon–size balls and place on greased baking sheets. Flatten slightly with a fork.

3. Bake 10 minutes, or until brown. Cool on rack.

4. Refrigerate in an airtight container for up to 2 weeks, or freeze indefinitely.

Makes 2–3 dozen small treats

* Choose plain baby food without onion powder. Note that the recipes in this book do not use garlic, which is in the same family as onions and is toxic to dogs.

Chewy Chicken Nuggets

Arrival Day Checklist

He trips over his ears when he runs. Her tummy is the warmest, softest thing you've ever touched. You've fallen in love. But wait! That bundle of joy's four legs will carry him into all kinds of trouble at home.

DO make advance arrangements with a vet for a check-up and vaccinations, if needed, if this has not already been done at the shelter. Make sure you are not bringing home a case of kennel cough, ear mites, or fleas!

DON'T pick up your new charge without first purchasing and setting up a good-size crate or kennel with room for a bed and food dishes (see Crate Training p. 78). Your pooch's new home should be in a warm, draft-free area away from heavy household traffic, possibly in your bedroom. Have ready a heater or hot-water bottle, and the proverbial ticking wind-up clock (to simulate Mom's heartbeat). Take a towel to the breeder, and rub Mom with it to take her scent home with you.

DO call ahead and find out what brand of food and treats your pooch has been eating. Even if you plan to make future adjustments, buy the same brand at first. Arrival day is not the time to make dietary changes.

DON'T take your own dishes out of the cupboard for your new arrival. Your pooch deserves his own (preferably stainless-steel) bowls. Discuss the appropriate size with your pet-supply owner.

DO get your dog's measurements and have a fairly short leash and comfortable harness on hand. Choker collars and extendable (uncontrollable) leashes are out. Do set up an extendable leash in an appropriate way, if you plan to stake your dog out in the yard.

DON'T allow your new charge to ride loose in the car. Use a carrier, crate, or buckle-down harness, and buckle the carrier in with a seat belt.

DO attend to household hazards before arrival day. This means anything your puppy might chew on or ingest, such as electrical cords, toxic foods, small toys and other objects, and even socks (see Puppyproofing Your Home, p. 168).

DON'T allow your pooch free run of the house upon arrival. This is the perfect way to encourage a potty accident. If your pooch is old enough, potty him outside on a leash before bringing him indoors. Be sure to reward him for doing his business outside—with a treat he's used to. Allow him to work off some nervous energy, and then introduce him immediately to his large, comfy crate.

DO try to keep your pup confined to one area at first, taking him out of the crate or room only for walks, bathroom breaks, and playtime. Feed her in her crate so she will regard it as her own happy home. Shelter animals will be especially thankful for this cozy abode. Don't pull your pup out of his crate—coax him out.

DON'T allow family members to tease the dog through the crate. Introduce your pup to the household and other pets gradually. Take special care to remind established pets and tiny family members how much you love them. Expect some jealous behavior!

DO shower your new family member with appropriate, puppy-safe toys.

DON'T ever leave an unattended, untrained puppy loose at home alone.

DOG RULES

1. The dog is not allowed in the house!

2. Okay, the dog is allowed in the house, but only in certain rooms.

3. The dog is allowed in all rooms, but has to stay off the furniture.

4. The dog can get on the OLD furniture only.

5. Fine, the dog is allowed on all the furniture, but is not allowed to sleep with the humans on the bed.

6. All right, the dog is allowed on the bed, but ONLY by invitation.

7. The dog can sleep on the bed whenever he wants, but NOT under the covers.

8. The dog can sleep under the covers by invitation ONLY.

9. The dog can sleep under the covers every night.

10. Humans must ask permission to sleep under the covers with the dog.

Dogs Vis-à-Vis Cats

by Roy Blount, Jr.

Which is the better pet, a cat or a dog?

Well, which is the better fruit, an apple or an orange?

Of dogs, in my time, I have had Sailor, Brownie, Bobby, Smokey, Butch, Snoopy (before "Peanuts"), Tubby, Sam, Chipper, Owen, Peggy, Ned, Sadie, Mollie and Pie. Of cats, I have had Stranger, Lulu, Angel, Emmy, Piedmont, Haile, Bale, Snope and Eloise. And Peggy's eight puppies and Eloise's two batches of kittens.

Down through the years, those hairy little entities have been parts of my life, nearly as intimate to me as my ankles. I have predominantly fond thoughts about every one of them, except possibly Smokey, who used to get lost and have to be bailed out of the pound all the time.

In the presence of all those names, I hate to generalize. Emmy acted a lot like a dog, and Tubby hung around happily with cats. You can't lump your pets together by their species any more than you can your friends by their professions. (I have known English professors who acted like people in the shrimping business.) But I'll tell you one thing. A cat can't smile. Or won't.

A dog will smile. Romp with your dog for a while and he or

she will beam. Light up. You tell me the expression on that dog's face is not a smile. A mule or a monkey or a porpoise will sort of grin, but a dog is the only animal that will *smile*.

I'm not saying a cat won't joke. One morning I came downstairs to find a whole, perfect, upright rabbit's head on the floor. It looked as though a rabbit had stuck its head up through the floor to take a look around. Only the head wasn't moving.

"Waughh!" was my first reaction. Then I realized that a perky-looking disembodied rabbit's head on the floor was Snope's or Eloise's idea of a joke. Neither of them would own up to it in any way, of course. Neither of them smiled. I love cats but . . . But I am always saying, "I love cats, but . . ."

A dog will make eye contact. A cat will, too, but a cat's eyes don't even look entirely warm-blooded to me, whereas a dog's eyes look human except less guarded. A dog will look at you as if to say, "What do you want me to do for you? I'll do anything for you." Whether a dog *can* in fact, do anything for you if you don't have sheep (I never have) is another matter. The dog is *willing*.

A cat will do something for you: a cat will mouse. But I'm not sure that a house free of mice is better off than a house free of kitty litter. (I hate kitty litter. Have you ever been washing your hands and had your wet bar of soap fall into the kitty litter? Or your toothbrush? In the morning?) And

a cat that mouses will also gerbil, parakeet, and rabbit.
Furthermore, a cat will not do any of these things because
you want him to.

I say that from experience and observation. I say it in the
face of recent comments by Dr. Michael W. Fox, the scien-
tific director of the Humane Society of the U.S. Fox main-
tains that he knows of cats that switch on lights, cats that
flush the toilet, cats that press the lever of an electric can
opener, and one cat that "knocks the tele-
phone off the hook when it rings, listens to
the receiver and meows into the mouth-
piece." He cites another cat that would
only take a pill "after its owner told it the
pill was important to take."

Okay. Okay. After its owner told it
the pill was *important to the cat*. You
won't find a cat that will do something because it means a great deal
to the owner.

When a cat makes eye contact
with a person, the cat's expression
says, "So?" There is little that a person can say in response to this
expression. Cats have not forgotten that
they were worshiped by the ancient

Egyptians. It went to their heads. A cat's eyes know what a cat's eyes know.

Dogs' eyes twinkle, well up, express yearning. Which may be why cats are fast overtaking dogs in popularity in American homes. Taking care of cats is less of a problem than taking care of dogs, and cats are less demanding *emotionally*. A dog will smile, and a dog will also look at you as if you have been abusing him because you have not kneaded the place where his ears join onto his head in the last ten minutes. "Is it something I did?" the dog's eyes ask. "Haven't I been a good enough dog to you? God knows you know I love you. Why don't you want to go out into the woods and watch me chase squirrels? You're breaking—I'm not *accusing* you. I know you must have a reason, but I'm just saying—you're breaking my heart." Having a dog in the home is too much like having a person. Having a cat in the home is not enough like having a person.

Robert Graves once said that he wrote novels for the money he needed to live so he could write poetry. His books of prose, he said, were the show dogs he raised to support his cat. I guess a cat is sort of like a poem. A cat is relatively short. A cat is only subtly demonstrative. To be sure, you can curl up with a good cat, but that doesn't mean you *understand* the cat. A dog is like Dickens. 🐾

Things Dogs Must Remember

- I will not play tug–of–war with Dad's underwear when he's on the toilet.

- The garbage collector is NOT stealing our stuff.

- I do not need to suddenly stand straight up when I'm lying under the coffee table.

- I must shake the rainwater out of my fur BEFORE entering the house.

- I will not eat the cats' food, before or after they eat it.

- I will not roll on dead birds, seagulls, fish, crabs, etc.

- The diaper pail is not a cookie jar.

- When in the car, I will not insist on having the window rolled down when it's raining outside.

- The sofa is not a face towel. Neither are Mom and Dad's laps.

- I will not take off while on the leash to chase squirrels while Mommy is standing on a slippery grass slope.

- I will not roll my toys behind the fridge.

The Dog Life Cycle

When does your pup cross the threshold into full-fledged "doggyhood"? Dog-show people will consider an animal a puppy through 12 months and often up to 18. Many dogs remain immature, in body and mind, throughout the first 24 months. Dogs age about 10 years to our 1 in their first 2 years, and about 4 or 6 "dog years" to each "human year" after that, depending on the breed. Large breeds like Great Danes and mastiffs tend to have life expectancies of less than 10 years, while some small breeds, like the Yorkshire terrier, can live into their 20s!

INFANCY Until about Day 20 of its life, a pup cannot see or hear. The mother is responsible for all cleaning and feeding duties. From Week 3 through 7, pups remain with their littermates, learning to act like dogs and becoming socialized by their mom and human caregivers. It's not wise to leave an entire litter together for much longer than 12 weeks, however; domineering/submissive behavior is heightened and can become a training issue later on. Even at this age, dividing the puppies' area into definite feeding, playing, sleeping, and elimination areas can facilitate housebreaking.

JUVENILE DELINQUENCY At around 7 weeks, a dog happily enters early childhood as a curious, wagging, mouthing, peeing pup who is everywhere at once and loves nothing more than your warm cuddles—not to mention 4 meals a day. First vaccinations are given by this point. At this stage, a pup has developed a controlled bite, or the ability to use the mouth and teeth without harm, has baby teeth, and begins showing signs of bowel control. Use a board to separate your pup's elimination area from his feeding area. Laying down newspaper with pine shavings on top for a potty will help him get the right idea. Feed your dog high-quality puppy food until she is at least a year old (see also How Much is Too Much?, p. 335).

For proper socialization, you must begin to expose the 7-to-26-week-old pup to all kinds of stimuli, including noise, handling, children, strangers, and other pets. Your young friend will be eager to please you, so remember to praise good manners effusively and consistently. Dogs who grow up with lots of praise for good behavior become well-adjusted adults.

TERRIBLE TEENS By 6 months, your pooch becomes a teenager and is mature enough to be "altered." Why spay or neuter? The ASPCA says that besides preventing unwanted puppies, spaying or neutering your dog before he or she reaches full sexual maturity helps prevent testicular cancer, prostate disease, pyometra (a serious infection of the uterus), and breast cancer. Spayed or neutered animals are better-behaved and lead longer, happier lives; remember that dogs who are not altered are constantly stressed by the urge to mate, and can become destructive in their efforts to get out.

It's time to address any serious behavioral problems that emerge—like severe separation anxiety, for example—in addition to the usual puppy mischief. Punishment, while it may

work on your teenage kids, may create its own set of new problems with your dog. If needed, start thinking about obedience school, where you and your dog can receive an education in positive techniques. Besides, if your teenage canine is well behaved, you are more likely to take her places, and she will be happier as a result.

MIDDLE YEARS Now you have that perfect canine companion you were hoping for. Someone to go to the store with, take long walks with—maybe even take to work and on vacation. He doesn't ask for much, except for a warm place to sleep, good food, and above all, your company. There is nothing like a dog's waggly tail to raise you up from the hardest day at work, the worst breakup, the most critical remark on the part of a friend. Make sure you repay him by keeping up with brushing, exercise, flea and heartworm control, good nutrition, and regular vet and dental checks.

SENIOR STATUS At 10, some breeds have several more years to go before they reach "retirement age." Indeed, statistics show that the average dog can live 14 years or more. Your older friend has proven to be as loyal as the best of humans. Reward him with a heated pet bed for that touch of arthritis. Don't ignore what you think are small ailments, like chronic stomach upset. A vet can screen for a vast array of problems in one routine blood test, and can address thyroid, kidney, and digestive issues early on. Pay special attention to keeping her on the correct diet for her age, weight, and teeth. And don't forget to give her extra affection, even if she's a little quieter than she used to be. After all, no one loves you like Man's Best Friend.

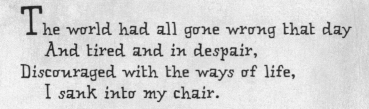

The world had all gone wrong that day
  And tired and in despair,
Discouraged with the ways of life,
  I sank into my chair.

A soft caress fell on my cheek,
  My hands were trust apart.
And two big sympathizing eyes
  Gazed down into my heart.

I had a friend; what cared I now
  For fifty worlds? I knew
One heart was anxious when I grieved—
  My dog's heart, loyal, true.

"God bless him," breathed I soft and low,
  And hugged him close and tight.
One lingering lick upon my ear
  And we were happy—quite.

My Comforter by Anonymous

51

Training 101

The domestication of dogs merely requires that they be tame; the socialization of a dog, however, requires her to inhibit her natural tendencies in order to share your home. Trainers believe that an untrained pooch is an unhappy, bored, confused and frustrated one. Even worse, an untrained dog who gets out of control or runs away can be injured.

Most mistakes are made in a pup's first days at home. If nothing else, bring your new pooch home to a crate, not the whole house. (Then reach for the phone and call that trainer.) **Do not allow a potty accident to occur**. Remove the dog immediately to the outdoors when taking him out of the crate so he can eliminate. Allowing the dog to soil the house, even once, is an invitation for a repeat disaster, and you will find it nearly impossible to teach him to "unlearn" that behavior. It's a costly error: People who leave an unsupervised, untrained dog loose in the house are unwittingly teaching the dog that it's okay to leave its calling card on the rugs and furniture.

If your dog has an accident and you deal with it by rubbing his nose in it, yelling, or swatting him, you are not teaching the dog that the behavior of toileting in the house is bad; you are telling him that you are upset about the mess. The poor dog will feel guilty but continue to potty in the house. The secret is, don't let it happen. It's possible to adopt and train a dog without ever having a single housebreaking error (see Housebreaking, p. 78).

Boot Camp for Dog Owners

You're now in basic training. And what do trainees learn? *Attitude.*

First, realize that biting, marking, chewing, barking, and chasing are normal doggy activities. You simply want your pooch to *limit* certain behaviors to certain places and times.

Also, remember, who is *really* in control? Who knows your rules? You do. Your dog does not. She will want to know, and you must find a way to tell her.

Most training methods have the same two aims: (1) to keep the dog from teaching himself undesirable behaviors; and (2) to condition the dog to engage in desirable ones, such as chewing on a Kong instead of your daughter's science project. The trend today is away from punishment and harsh "corrections" and toward positive reinforcement and—especially with dogs— prevention of unacceptable behaviors in the first place. The *tools* used by these methods are many.

*Sharing your life with a dog requires a huge commitment. Here's a sensible piece of tough love: If you love cute puppies but do not have the time to train, train, train, then—**please**— seriously consider getting a stuffed animal instead, until you are ready.*

The dog
is a yes—
animal.
Very
popular
with
people
who can't
afford a
yes—man.

—ROBERTSON DAVIES

Let's Hit the Road

by Maya Gottfried

Listen up! It's time to go.

Get the leash. Let's hit the road.

I've got a bone to pick with a Chihuahua,

And there's a coupla dachshunds that

   need a barking-to.

Put down your paper already,

   let's get this show on the road.

Throw me my stick,

I'm ready to go.

Owney the U.S. Mail Dog

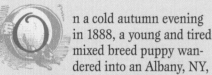

O n a cold autumn evening in 1888, a young and tired mixed breed puppy wandered into an Albany, NY, post office to escape the cold. He bedded there comfortably on a pile of old mailbags and did not move till daybreak. The postal staff noticed the intruder but chose to let him sleep. When the pup awoke, the staff fed and welcomed him as their new pet. The pup, named "Owney" by the staff, proved quite friendly and intelligent and quickly transformed from a homeless mutt into the proud mascot of the entire United States Postal Service.

During his adjustment to his new surroundings, Owney became attached to the odor and feel of old mailbags as well as everyone who carried their scent. One day he accompanied a mail cart loaded with shipments to the local rail depot, followed a mail shipment from the cart into a railcar, and enjoyed the ride all the way to New York City. The crew on the receiving end sent him back on a returning train. The Albany staff soon noticed that Owney was frequently absent and realized that he enjoyed traveling. Eventually the duration of Owney's trips grew, and the postal staff bought a collar to identify him in case of an emergency. The collar read: "Owney, Post Office, Albany, New York."

Owney traveled throughout the country, hopping from train to train and receiving food, shelter, and the companionship of postal employees everywhere, yet he always returned to his Albany home base. The Albany crew attached a message to Owney's collar requesting that all who meet him record his travels and attach their own messages. Soon, his collar sagged with the weight of metal tags marking his stops. As a result, the Postmaster General John Wanamaker himself presented Owney with a special harness to better wield his souvenirs. Owney trav-eled so frequently, his network of assistants lightened his load by rotat-ing the memorabilia and returning it to his Albany base for posterity.

Owney's travels took him through the continental United States, Canada, Mexico, and Alaska. On August 19, 1895, he stowed away on the steamship Victoria, traveling to Asia, where he was given royal treat-ment and issued an imperial passport for travel throughout Japan. From there, he sailed around the world, visiting Singapore, Suez,

59

Algiers, and the Azores. Then he returned to New York City, and finally went on to Tacoma, Washington. The trip took a total of 132 days and over 143,000 miles.

Owney became an international sensation and was invited to many dog shows where he received "Globe Trotter" awards and other honors. In 1897, Owney's caretakers decided that he was too old for such extensive travel, as he suffered numerous health problems. However, his wanderlust prevailed—he slipped from their sight and boarded a mail train bound for Ohio. While in Toledo, a postal clerk introduced Owney to a newspaper reporter. Although the circumstances surrounding the incident are unclear, it was reported that Owney became ill tempered and was shot. He passed

away in Toledo on June 11, 1897. Distraught at their loss, mail clerks raised funds to have Owney preserved, and he was given to the Post Office Department's headquarters in Washington, D.C.

Today, Owney remains an admired international symbol of adventure. His preserved body has rested in the Smithsonian Institution since 1911. He was the one and only dog to ever be adopted by the U.S. Postal Service. 🐾

Playtime!

Playtime allows the opportunity get to know your pup's subtler traits and helps induct her into the family. These games not only provide entertainment but help in managing behavior as well. But don't forget: the fun is the true goal!

HIDE-AND-SEEK FOR TREATS Play this game alone in the house with your dog, or with a partner or family members. If your dog does a very good sit, put her in a sit while you or the others hide. Then release her by saying "okay," or have partners call her to them one at a time and give her a treat when she finds them. Use either her normal "recall" cue or just her name. Some dogs will use their noses for this, and others will use sight. Most will learn a more reliable recall.

KEEPAWAY A combination of Battle Ball and Pickle in the Middle, this out-door activity requires two or more people. Shake a soft, flabby rubber ball in the dog's face to get him interested. Whip the ball back and forth among people, all the while trying to keep the ball away from the energetic pooch, who will be racing after you and snapping at it. Each time Fido intercepts a pass and catches the ball, the thrower is out. Don't make it too hard. Doggie always wins!

CLEAN UP YOUR TOYS This is great for a dog who likes to bring you "gifts." Use a basket to store dog toys, or simply use the area around your dog's bed. When she brings you a toy, say, "Clean up your toys," and gesture at the bed or basket. Each time she gets the toy near the area, reward her with a food treat. Some dogs make the leap and start dropping things directly into the container.

KONG Invented in 1976 by KONG for dogs, the stuffable, chewable, hard-rubber toy that comes in many variations, Kong has become a household word. Many a shoe collection has been saved by Kongs! Recommended universally by behaviorists, the Kong Original, Dental Kong, Kong Stuff-a-Ball, Goodie Ship, and Training Dummy are must-haves. Kong paste and kibble go inside, or use your own.

Pooch Playtime
Top Ten Dog Toys

KONG AIR DOG TOYS In a category for the aeronautically inclined pooch, the Air Dog Kong, Air Dog Doughnut, and Flying Squirrel Kong (whose feet spin in the air) are a few of these lightweight, easy-to-catch outdoor toys.

SNUGGLEPUPPIE A combination pillow and companion for a new pup or older dog, the SnugglePuppie is so adorable you may just have to get one for yourself. A heater and heartbeat simulator in a special compartment will help your furry child drift right off to sleep.

FRISBEE The list would not be complete without it! "Canine disc sports" are a growing pastime. The Hyperflite Skyhoundz Canine Disc Championships (www.skyhoundz.com/competition.htm) range from local to world levels. Frisbee and other manufacturers now make special doggy discs.

GENTLE LEADER You didn't think this doubled as a toy, but your dog does! Gentle Leader's collar and leash designs are tops for walkies. Hide it, or your pup will keep bringing it to you.

BALL LAUNCHERS Fling that ball farther! Chuckit and HyperDog provide small, portable solutions to a sore throwing arm. For the truly ball-obsessed dog, there's the pricier, remote-controlled GoDogGo. Teach your dog to load it with up to 15 tennis balls; custom-set it from your patio chair.

DR. NOYS PLUSH TOYS This beautiful, nearly indestructible line of plush toys gets everyone's vote because the squeaker inside is replaceable—and an extra one comes with each toy. Choose from chipmunks, ducks, snakes, and bunnies, among others, in all sizes.

TUG-N-TOSS JOLLY BALL An all-time favorite of dogs who like to latch on and play tug of war, these durable, soft rubber balls in various sizes have handles. Great for teaching your dog to bite toys, not hands.

"GENUINE IMITATION" SHEEPSKIN TUG This 20-inch tugger has squeakers in the ends. It's hilarious to watch two dogs play with it together.

TALKING TOYS The latest craze, these have a computer chip inside that allows you to record your own voice. Try the plush Talking Bone or the Talk-to-Me Laser Treat Ball. Ours would say, "Stay off the couch!"

A Dog's Life

by Peter Mayle

One lesson I've learned in life is that everything is negotiable. No crime, however foul, is beyond redemption. You can steal the Sunday lunch, shred books, bit off the heads of live chickens, and pretty much despoil to your heart's contents as long as your conciliation technique is sound. It's known as plea bargaining, and it has allowed far worse villains than I to walk away unpunished, with scarcely a blot on their escutcheon. If you don't believe me, read the newspapers.

Punishment in our house, as in the legal system generally, depends not only on the gravity of the offense but also—and this is possibly more important—on the mood and general disposition of the presiding judge and the jury. There are days when a petty misdemeanor can lead to physical retribution and temporary exile; on other occasions, all you get for the same infringement is a verbal warning and half an hour's probation, with remission for good behavior. A tricky thing, justice. You can never tell which way it's going to jump.

The atmosphere on this particular evening was fraught. I suspect it was not merely the nature of the crime but also the effects of an excessive lunch, which often come to the surface in the early part of the evening: nagging headache, dyspepsia, and bloat, accompanied by short temper. The judge was going to go for the maximum sentence, in my estimation, and so I decided to hold nothing back. The full repertoire was called for. It was time for some advanced body dynamics, or what I prefer to call the "seven gestures of appeasement." I pass them on to you in the hope that you never need to use them.

ONE

Roll over on the back, after the fashion of the cocker spaniel, and wave the legs helplessly. This serves to indicate remorse and to foil the first instinct of the angry human, which is to administer painful blows to the hindquarters. You cannot smack them at floor level with any degree of force.

TWO

The tone of voice will tell you when the heat of the moment has subsided and it's safe to get up and approach the judge and jury. This should be done with the modified shimmy—head down in shame, with the rest of the body wriggling in a frenzy of apology. Soft, contrite sounds are appropriate here if you have the knack of making them. Avoid barking or any baring of the teeth.

THREE

Sit. Raise the right paw and place on the nearest available knee. For some reason, most people consider this endearing, and the chances of a clip around the ear are remote.

FOUR

Remove the paw and rest the full weight of the head on the chosen knee. In most cases, this will provoke an involuntary pat, and then you know you're home and dry. If it doesn't work, proceed with the rest of the program.

FIVE

Establish the whereabouts of a hand. After making sure that it isn't holding a glass of red wine, butt it with a firm upward motion of the head. I mention the red wine only because of an unfortunate accident that I was once blamed for, quite unfairly, which rather spoiled the magic of the moment.

SIX

By now, all should be forgiven, but it's important to be seen not to celebrate too quickly. I always take the time for a few tender minutes of affectionate leaning—against a leg or an arm, whichever is most convenient. The appendage doesn't matter; it's the endearing gesture that is vital.

And that, nine times out of ten, should do the trick. Only in desperate situations, when every blandishment has met with grim rebuff and hideous threats persist, do I have to resort to the ultimate solution and unleash my secret weapon.

I should explain the history of it. Some years ago, one of my admirers presented me with a life-size replica of the traditional Christmas cracker in bright red rubber, with festive green sprigs of rubber holly at either end, a definite collector's piece. It happens to be a very satisfying object to hold in the mouth; well-shaped and with just the right amount of give. You've probably never held the upper part of a squirrel's back leg between your teeth. I have, and my cracker has a similar consistency. Firm but yielding, if you follow me. The other similarity to the squirrel is that my cracker squeaks when bitten. This amuses me, and for reasons that I couldn't begin to explain, it makes people laugh. Never fails. And so, in extremis, when catastrophe looms, do I give up and wait for my just deserts? Do I cower under the withering gaze of disapproval? Certainly not. I fetch my cracker.

SEVEN

Even here, a certain delicacy of tough is necessary. Constant squeaking irritates the human ear, as I've noticed many times when the television is on, and so I sit with cracker clenched between the teeth, looking as forlorn as possible, and squeak at irregular intervals. And, what do you know, it always works. Always. Heaven knows why, but within seconds the storm clouds disappear and I am restored to grace, thanks to the squeak that turns away wrath. There's a lesson here somewhere for mankind, and if you ever find yourself involved in litigation, my advice is to make sure you have a rubber cracker in your pocket.

EIGHT

Recognize the need for selective obedience. Under normal circumstances, you can do more or less what you like. Man's innate idleness and short attention span will save you from too much discipline. But there will be moments of crisis when it pays to respond to a call from the authorities. You can always tell. Voices are raised, hysteria looms, and threats are uttered. When they shout in capital letters—as in "BOY! DAMNIT!"—return to base immediately, pretending you didn't hear the first time. Wag sincerely, and all will be well.

NINE

Finally, remember that we live in an imperfect world. People make mistakes. Cocktail parties, pale-colored furniture, hair transplants, New Year's Eve, working tablets, vibrant orange Lycra, diamanté dog collars, jogging, grooming, telephone sex, leg waxing—the list is long, and life is short. My advice is to make the best of it, and to make allowances. To err is human. To forgive, canine. 🐾

He's a Very Smart Dog

I went to the movies the other day and in the front row was an old man and his dog. It was a sad, funny kind of film. In the sad part, the dog cried his eyes out, and in the funny part, the dog laughed its head off. This happened all the way through the film. After the film had ended, I decided to go and speak to the man.

"That's the most amazing thing I've seen," I said. "That dog really seemed to enjoy the film."

The man turned to me and said, "Yeah, it is. He hated the book."

An Amazin' Mutt

A man and his dog walk into a bar. The man proclaims, "I'll bet you a round of drinks that my dog can talk."

"Yeah! Sure... go ahead," says the bartender.

"What covers a house?" asks the man.

"Roof!" answers the dog.

"How does sandpaper feel?" asks the man.

"Rough!" answers the dog.

"Who was the greatest ball player of all time?" asks the man.

"Ruth!"

"Pay up. I told you he could talk," says the man.

The bartender, annoyed, throws both of them out the door. Sitting on the sidewalk, the dog looks at the man and says, "or is the greatest player Mantle?"

KIBBLE DRIBBLE One of the best treats is a piece of high-quality dry food that is different from your dog's usual fare. You can purchase these or bake them for your dog from the Little Big Book recipes that follow. Some toys are designed to dispense dry treats while your dog plays (see Top Ten Dog Toys, p. 64). Trainers like kibble because the smell emanating from their hands and clothing is less distracting to the dog.

Fido's Favorites
Tips for Using Treats

ODOR ISSUES Dogs learn early on that the smell of food precedes eating, and so they can be led to think that the intense smell of meat must be present for them to follow a command. If you are trying to teach your dog obedience and you smell like a delicatessen, then the dog can become confused when you give her a command without the smell! So, if you are training with food, vary your treats.

PEANUT BUTTER Peanut butter ranks as one of the most sought-after and nutritious treats a dog can get his lips around, but how do you dispense this gooey delicacy? Load a Kong with plain, unsalted PB and put it in the freezer (see Top Ten Dog Toys, p. 64). Give it to your pooch and watch her go to town. It's a great way to keep a pup busy—and discourage her from jumping on your guests—for a good half hour. Stuffed Kongs also make a perfect solution for separation issues. Give one to an anxious dog as you head out for the day, and hide a few others around the house to keep him out of trouble. Another Kong stuffer is cream cheese or cheese softened in a microwave.

TREAT BEAT Treats are often the backbone of training. At first, you will want to treat your dog each time he obeys you. Eventually, you should give treats at random intervals while asking your dog to repeat a behavior, sometimes offering only praise. Fido gets a treat, but he never knows when, and that makes him want to obey you even more! It's important for a dog's own safety that he learn to obey basic commands, even when there's no food handy. You never know when a dangerous situation might arise, such as a car backing out of a driveway, and you need your dog to heel or come to you. Remember to treat your dog when you get back home!

DELI RAGE

Hot-dog bits are an oft-used training treat, and dogs go crazy over them. Keep in mind, though, that their sodium content is very high. Cut these up into tiny morsels and use them sparingly.

Birch
by Karen Shepard

You gonna eat that?
You gonna eat that?
You gonna eat that?

I'll eat that.

Housebreaking Your New Arrival

Housebreaking is the number one problem that dog owners complain about, but the problem lies with a lack of understanding on the part of the owner, not with the dog. Good potty habits in a dog come about only as a result of training and good communication.

There are several ways to housebreak an animal, all requiring that you devote some time to being with your pet.

Potty accidents occur because people are reluctant to train their dogs; but take heart: Dogs take to clicker training and other gentle methods better than just about any other animal. Some people even condition their dogs to use a litter box! If you've ever seen a service dog curb itself along a busy city street, then you know how trainable dogs are. Responsible dog owners are finding that it's best to take the time to teach their dogs basic obedience. The key is consistency.

Remember: Puppies need to relieve themselves about six times per day, and should be taken out right after each meal. Never leave an untrained puppy at home unattended.

Crate Training

This may be the fastest, easiest housebreaking method ever invented, but it requires a commitment to doing it *correctly*. Usually taking only a few days, the method involves leaving your dog in his crate with his bed and food, and taking him out only on a schedule. Do not reward whining by letting the dog out. If she potties when you take her outside (or to a litter box or pad), reward her: Provide treats, extensive

playtime, and a nice long walk before putting her back in the crate. Crate training must be balanced with sufficient periods of exercise and companionship; long periods in crate isolation are detrimental. Work on extending the amount of supervised time out of the crate.

If she doesn't potty when you take her out, put her back in the crate. Stay on schedule. Normally, a dog will not "soil its nest." If you work all day, you must get someone to take the dog out during this training; a dog left in a crate becomes neurotic and destructive.

Once the training seems to have "taken," let the dog out and confine him to the room (with a washable floor), continuing the potty schedule. Keep an eye on the pooch; if he shows signs of getting ready to pee or poop (like sniffing or turning in circles), say "Ah-ah!" and *immediately* take him out—do not take the time to get your coat! If accidents occur, backtrack to the crate. Do not yell at or punish your dog: Traditional forms of punishment don't teach him anything and will confuse him. Your dog does not understand what you disapprove of if you yell at him after the act. He will feel guilty about the mess, but he will keep doing it because he does not connect the mess with the act.

The dog must learn to think of your house as a nest he must not soil. A crate-trained puppy often will never have an accident—he learns that the only place to do his business is outside, or where you take him, and that pottying correctly is fun because it brings rewards. A dog allowed to eliminate around the house will take longer to learn, but this is the best way to end it. Be patient and consistent.

Eliminate on Command

Clicker trainers, professionals, and people with disabilities often use this method, which requires the dog to signal you when she has to go out. If your dog has some very basic training in pooping outdoors, you can easily condition her to ring a bell tied to the back door when she has to go. After all, it's more fun to ring the bell and go outside than it is to poop in the house. Show her the bell, get her to paw it, immediately give her a treat, and let her out. Once your dog does her business, don't run inside—reward her with playtime, praise, and treats **after** she goes. That way, she learns to potty right away, and not take her time about it.

Pads

If you must be away all day, use housebreaking pads in the room where the dog is confined (after the initial crate period), and use the crate at night. Set up the pads far away from the dog's food, water, and bed. Strengthen your dog's conditioning by taking him to the pad after meals, during potty breaks, and whenever he shows signs of having to go.

Paper

Not as highly recommended as pads, newspapers can be used as long as you keep the stack in the same exact spot. Encourage your pet by leading her from her crate to the papers. Once your pooch uses the stack, remove and replace the top layers but leave the rest; your dog will detect a slight urine smell that will lead her to that spot for pottying.

The Love-Master
From White Fang

by Jack London

Weedon Scott had set himself the task of redeeming White Fang —or rather, of redeeming mankind from the wrong it had done White Fang. It was a matter of principle and conscience. He felt that the ill done White Fang was a debt incurred by man, and that it must be paid. So he went out of his way to be especially kind to the Fighting Wolf. Each day he made it a point to caress and pet White Fang, and to do it at length.

At first suspicious and hostile, White Fang grew to like this petting. But there was one thing that he never out-grew—his growling. Growl he would, from the moment the petting began till it ended. But it was a growl with a new note in it. A stranger could not hear this note, and to such a stranger the growling of White Fang was an exhibition of primordial savagery, nerve-racking and blood-curdling. But White Fang's throat had become harsh-fibred from the mak-ing of ferocious sounds through the many years since his first little rasp of anger in the lair of his cubhood, and he could not soften the sounds of that throat now to express the gentleness he felt. Nevertheless, Weedon Scott's ear and sympathy were fine enough to catch the new note all but

drowned in the fierceness—the note that was the faintest hint of a croon of content and that none but he could hear.

As the days went by, the evolution of *like* into *love* was accelerated. White Fang himself began to grow aware of it, though in his consciousness he knew not what love was. It manifested itself to him as a void in his being—a hungry, aching, yearning void that clamored to be filed. It was a pain and an unrest, and it received easement only by the touch of the new god's presence. At such times love was a joy to him—a wild, keen-thrilling satisfaction. But when away from his god the pain and the unrest returned; the void in him sprang up and pressed against him with its emptiness, and the hunger gnawed and gnawed unceasingly.

White Fang was in the process of finding himself. In spite of the maturity of his years and of the savage rigidity of the mould that had formed him, his nature was undergoing an expansion. There was a burgeoning within him of strange feelings and unwonted impulses. His old code of conduct was changing. In the past he had liked comfort and surcease from pain. Disliked discomfort and pain and he had adjusted his actions accordingly. But now it was different.

Because of this new feeling within him he ofttimes elected discomfort and pain for the sake of his god. Thus, in the early morning, instead of roaming and foraging or lying in a sheltered nook, he would wait for hours on the cheerless cabin-stoop for a sight of the god's face. At night, when the god returned home, White Fang would leave the warm sleeping-place he had burrowed in the snow in order to receive the friendly snap of fingers and the word of greeting. Meat, even meat itself, he would forgo to be with his god, to receive a caress from him, or to accompany him down into the town.

Like had been replaced by *love*. And love was the plummet dropped down into the deeps of him where like had never gone. And responsive out of his deeps had come the new thing—love. That which was given unto him did he return. This was a god indeed, a love-god, a warm and radiant god, in whose light White Fang's nature expanded as a flower expands under the sun.

But White Fang was not demonstrative. He was too old, too firmly moulded, to become adept at expressing himself in new ways. He was too self-possessed, too strongly poised in his own isolation. Too long had he cultivated reticence, aloofness, and moroseness. He had never barked in his life, and he could not now learn to bark a welcome when his god approached. He was never in the way, never extravagant nor foolish in the expression of his love. He never ran to meet his god. He waited at a distance; but he always waited, was always there. His love partook of the nature of worship—dumb, inarticulate, a silent adoration. Only by the steady regard of his eyes did he express his love, and by the unceasing following with his eyes of his god's every movement. Also, at times, when his god looked at him and spoke to him, he betrayed an awkward self-consciousness, caused by the struggle of his love to express itself and his physical inability to express it.

He learned to adjust himself in many ways to his new mode of life. It was borne in upon him that he must let his master's dogs alone. Yet his dominant nature asserted itself, and he had first to thrash them into an acknowledgment of his superiority and leadership. This accomplished, he had little trouble with them. They gave trail to him when he came and went or walked among them, and when he asserted his will they obeyed.

In the same way, he came to tolerate Matt—as a possession of his master. His master rarely fed him. Matt did that—it was his business; yet White Fang divined that it was his master's food he ate, and that it was his master who thus fed him vicariously. Matt it was who tried to put him into the harness and make him haul sled with the other dogs. But Matt failed. It was not until Weedon Scott put the harness on White Fang and worked him that he understood. He took it as his master's will that Matt should drive him and work him, just as he drove and worked his master's other dogs. . . .

In the late spring a great trouble came to White Fang. Without warning, the love-master disappeared. There had been warning, but White Fang was unversed in such things, and did not understand the packing of a grip. He remem-

bered afterwards that this packing had preceded the master's disappearance; but at the time he suspected nothing. That night he waited for the master to return. At midnight the chill wind that blew drove him to shelter at the rear of the cabin. There he drowsed, only half asleep, his ears keyed for the first sound of the familiar step. But, at two in the morning, his anxiety drove him out to the cold front stoop, where he crouched and waited.

But no master came. In the morning the door opened and Matt stepped outside. White Fang gazed at him wistfully. There was no common speech by which he might learn what he wanted to know. The days came and went, but never the master. White Fang, who had never known sickness in his life, became sick. He became very sick—so sick that Matt was finally compelled to bring him inside the cabin. Also, in writing to his employer, Matt devoted a postscript to White Fang.

Weedon Scott, reading the letter down in the Circle City, came upon the following:

'That damn wolf won't work. Won't eat. Ain't got no spunk left. All the dogs is licking him. Wants to know what has become of you, and I don't know how to tell him. Mebbe he is going to die.'

It was as Matt had said. White Fang had ceased eating, lost heart, and allowed every dog of the team to thrash him. In the cabin he lay on the floor near the stove, without

interest in food, in Matt, nor in life. Matt might talk gently
to him or swear at him, it was all the same; he never did
more than turn his dull eyes upon the man, then drop his
head back to its customary position on his fore-paws.

And then, one night, Matt, reading to himself with moving lips and mumbled sounds, was startled by a low whine
from White Fang. He had got upon his feet, his ears cocked
toward the door, and he was listening intently. A moment
later Matt heard a footstep. The door opened, and Weedon
Scott stepped in. The two men shook hands. Then Scott
looked around the room.

"Where's the wolf?" he asked.

Then he discovered him, standing where he had been
lying, near to the stove. He had not rushed forward after the
manner of other dogs. He stood, watching and waiting.

"Holy smoke!" Matt exclaimed. "Look at 'm wag his tail!"

Weedon Scott strode half across the room toward him, at
the same time calling him. White Fang came to him, not
with a great bound, yet quickly. He was awkward from self-
consciousness, but as he drew near his eyes took on a
strange expression. Something, an incommunicable vastness
of feeling, rose up into his eyes as a light shone forth.

"He never looked at me that way all the time you was
gone," Matt commented.

Weedon Scott did not hear. He was squatting down on his
heels, face to face with White Fang, and petting him—rubbing

at the roots of the ears, making long caressing strokes down the neck to the shoulders, tapping the spine gently with the balls of his fingers. And White Fang was growling responsively, the crooning note of the growl more pronounced than ever.

But that was not all. What of his joy, the great love in him, ever surging and struggling to express itself, succeeding in finding a new mode of expression? He suddenly thrust his head forward and nudged his way in between the master's arm and body. And here confined, hidden from view all except his ears, no longer growling, he continued to nudge and snuggle.

The two men looked at each other. Scott's eyes were shining.

"Gosh!" said Matt in an awe-stricken voice.

A moment later, when he had recovered himself, he said: "I always insisted that wolf was a dog. Look at 'm!"

With the return of the love-master, White Fang's recovery was rapid. Two nights and a day he spent in the cabin. Then he sallied forth. The sled-dogs had forgotten his prowess. They remembered only the latest, which was his weakness and sickness. At the sight of him as he came out of the cabin, they sprang upon him.

"Talk about your rough-houses," Matt murmured gleefully, standing in the doorway and looking on. "Give 'm hell, you wolf! Give 'm hell!—an' then some!"

White Fang did not need the encouragement. The return of the love-master was enough. Life was flowing through him again, splendid and indomitable. He fought from sheer joy, finding in it an expression of much that he felt and that otherwise was without speech. There could be but one ending. The team dispersed in ignominious defeat, and it was not until after dark that the dogs came sneaking back, one by one, by meekness and humility signifying their fealty to White Fang. 🐾

Man And Dog
by Siegfried Sassoon

Who's this—alone with stone and sky?
It's only my old dog and I—
It's only him; it's only me;
Alone with stone and grass and tree.

What share we most—we two together?
Smells, and awareness of the weather.
What is it makes us more than dust?
My trust in him; in me his trust.

Here's anyhow one decent thing
That life to man and dog can bring;
One decent thing, remultiplied
Till earth's last dog and man have died.

Dog Agility

Dogs love to run obstacle courses, whether they're backyard playgrounds or regulation setups. In fact, obstacle-course running is serious business. Browse the United States Dog Agility Association's Web page at www.usdaa.com to learn the rules and get ideas. A book of construction plans for USDAA agility obstacles—ranging from the A-frame and dog walk to the see-saw, tunnels, and hurdles—is available in their online store. Here's a do-it-yourself version of some obstacles, just for fun:

- Non-regulation tunnels: cardboard cartons opened and duct-taped together, or a fabric collapsible tunnel made for children
- Weave poles: traffic cones or plungers set in a row for your pooch to weave through slalom-style
- Hurdle: broomstick in notched cardboard cartons at each end
- Pedestal: any sturdy crate
- Ramped table: a splinter-free plank secured to a table and a cushion for the landing at the other end

Set it up in any order. At first, you may find it easiest to lure your dog through the course with food. Agility trainers "backchain" a series of obstacles together, by starting with the end obstacle first, to get the dog to run the entire course without hesitation. Your dog will learn what you want simply by repeating the course many times. It is great exercise.

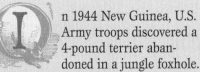

Smokey the Mascot Soldier

In 1944 New Guinea, U.S. Army troops discovered a 4-pound terrier abandoned in a jungle foxhole. Corporal Bill Wynne adopted the small dog and named her Smokey. In addition to surviving 150 air raids and serving as a crew member on twelve air-and-sea rescues during her service in New Guinea, Smokey performed tricks for the troops. She played dead, climbed ladders, walked a tightrope made of airplane scraps, and spelled her name with cardboard letters. She also performed an act of heroism. A communications wire needed to be strung through a pipe 8 inches high and 70 feet long beneath the airstrip of an allied airfield. The crew, stumped as to how to accomplish the task, requested Smokey's service and attached a string to her collar as a guide for the wire. Smokey hesitated, but then plunged into the darkness and triumphantly emerged at the other end of the dusty pipe after several tense moments without ever disrupting air traffic. For a decade after the war, Bill and Smokey continued to share her talents with the world. Smokey became the world's earliest documented therapy dog, presenting amusing feats at hospitals and entertaining children at orphanages. Smokey performed her tricks with Bill on stage and live television—sealing her fame in show business as one of the first dogs to appear on TV. 🐾

Sleeping with the Pack

by Michael J. Rosen

Dog-care books preach about allowing the dog, as a key member of your social pack, to sleep near you—if not *on* the bed (various studies suggest that more than 40 percent of us share our beds with canines), then at least somewhere in the bedroom or within monitoring, sniffing distance. Such physical proximity is crucial for packs where the humans are gone much of the day. The long nocturnal stretch reinforces the security that pack identity provides.

At this house, both humans are fortunate to work from home most days, living as part of the pack both day and night—yet I still appreciate the notion that my dogs inhale my scent while I'm asleep. To my dogs, I must possess a distinct complex of odors, even though to my nose this individual aroma is as ineffable as the very idea of "home." (Home, in fact, is the very quality that our sleeping together stockpiles for those hours they're alone in the physical house without "home"—meaning, their two humans).

But beyond fulfilling that important pack need, this sleeping arrangement provides comforts more crucial than a perfectly clean comforter. There are few forces as strong as a sleeping dog's gravity: the pull to lie next to your own dog in bed or in a square of winter sunlight on the floor, to yield to that tug of drowsiness as you stroke the fur of a large dog dozing tranquilly.

Even if my role is alpha male, I like this puppy mode, snuggling against a dog's curved back, pressing my chest against the heat-radiant fur, lolling an arm across the dog's rising and falling chest, and breathing more slowly, inhaling whatever cypress, clover, or musk smells merge in the coat. Aside from the walks we take together, the four of us burrowed in our bedroom den provides the headiest, most potent sense of our pack.

Though I've forgotten most of my short-lived time in medical school, I remember the words *hypnogogic* and *hypnopompic*: the state of going to sleep and the state of waking up. But knowing words for the bookends of dreams provides a handle, perhaps a legitimacy, to these two states that I most love to share with dogs. There are further reasons.

First, there is the heat I love, the dog's pre-warming of a chilly bed through the covers, as well as the dog's own insulating warmth above the blankets.

There's the security of their watchfulness even in sleep. As subconsciously as they continue to scrutinize the nuances of each noise for anything that might warrant rousing into an alarm, I, too, on some unconscious level, must take in their guarding presence as I sleep. It's the same invisible trust we cede the motion detectors' superior knowledge.

And there's their sheer weight. Recently an acquaintance wrote about acquiring her first Papillon (she'd bred the substantial Portuguese Water Spaniel most of her life): "You really must get *another* dog, a small one, for backup, just for sleeping. You don't know what it's like to wake up with a dog in bed." I replied immediately: "Ah, but *you* don't know what it's like to fumble into consciousness thinking that you've lost the use of your lower extremities, trying to piece together dream fragments . . . *Was there an accident? What happened? I couldn't have . . .* before realizing that your ninety-pound dog and your seventy-five-pound dog are stretched on either side of your body, anchoring the covers across your legs the way the Lilliputians restrained Gulliver." Still, I love that security.

What's more, dogs rarely mind your joining them at rest. Nor do they often refuse the request to stop whatever else they might have been doing to join you for a rest. People aren't as accommodating; we're fidgety, physically and psychologically. Human naps are usually taken solo.

Finally, there is the sound of these three other breaths that I love—growing longer and more plangent as their sleeps deepen. Even the occasional snores and twitches are reassuring. And, perhaps best of all, I love to wake and find the bedroom windows fogged or even glazed with ice from the condensation of our four breaths, before beginning whatever breathless schedule the new day has brought. 🐾

Doggy Dictionary

BATH A process by which the humans drench the floor, walls, and themselves. You can help by shaking vigorously and frequently.

BICYCLES Two-wheeled exercise machines invented for dogs to control body fat. To get maximum aerobic benefit hide behind a bush and dash out, bark loudly, and run alongside for a few yards. The person then swerves, falls into the bushes, and you prance away.

BUMP The best way to get your human's attention when they are drinking a fresh cup of coffee or tea.

DEAFNESS A malady that affects dogs when their person wants them to come in and they want to stay out. Symptoms include staring blankly at the person, running in the opposite direction, or lying down.

DOG BED Any soft, clean surface, such as the white bedspread in the guest room or the newly upholstered couch in the living room.

DROOL What you do when your people have food and you don't. To do this properly you must sit as close as you can and look sad and let the drool fall to the floor, or better yet, on their laps.

GARBAGE CAN A container which your neighbors put out once a week to test your ingenuity. You must stand on your hind legs and try to push the lid off with your nose. If you do it right you are rewarded with margarine wrappers to shred, beef bones to consume, and moldy crusts of bread.

LEASH A strap which attaches to your collar, enabling you to lead your person where you want him or her to go.

LOVE A feeling of intense affection, given freely and without restriction. The best way you can show your love is to wag your tail. If you're lucky, a human will love you in return.

SNIFF A social custom to use when you greet other dogs. Place your nose as close as you can to the other dog's rear end and inhale deeply, repeat several times, or until your person makes you stop.

SOFA Thing that is to dogs like a napkin is to people. After eating, it is polite to run up and down the front of the sofa to wipe your whiskers clean.

THUNDER A signal that the world is coming to an end. Humans remain amazingly calm during thunderstorms, so it is necessary to warn them of the danger by trembling uncontrollably, panting, rolling your eyes wildly, and following at their heels.

WASTEBASKET A dog toy filled with paper, envelopes, and old candy wrappers. When you get bored, turn over the basket and strew the papers all over the house until your person comes home.

Helping the Medicine Go Down

The vet prescribes a medication for your dog and effort-lessly demonstrates by giving her the first dose in the clinic office. It looked so easy, but you just can't seem to get the hang of it and you know a struggle is ahead.

Don't feel bad. At the vet's, your dog was intimidated into submission by the strange environment and a funny-smelling authority figure. Now that she's home, it's normal for her to resort to her usual feisty self. Regain some control by placing your dog on a table, if possible.

You or an assistant should put an arm around the dog and hold her snugly against your (their) body. Don't hold your dog's head up too high. Pull the upper jaw up while shoving the pill as far in as possible with your other hand. Quickly close the jaws and hold them shut until you see swallowing. If your dog won't swallow, blow in her face.

For a dog without a muzzle, cradle the back of the head in your hand or arm, as you would a cat, instead of grabbing the upper jaw. Squeeze the mouth open from the sides while pulling the jaw down with the other hand, and poke the pill in.

With liquid medicine, hold the dog's mouth shut. Work the medicine dropper in between the teeth at the side of the mouth, being careful not to scrape the gums. After depressing the plunger, continue to hold her jaws shut as she swallows it.

Hiding a pill in a ball of food is fine—as long as the dog eats it at once—but don't try this with liquids. There's no way to know if she got the entire dose.

Poor Rover
by Langston Hughes

Rover was in clover
With a bone
On the front lawn—
But Rover's fun was over
When his bone
Was gone.
Poor Rover!

Power Source
by Edward Field

Like harnessing
the tides or the wind,
how about attaching
dogs' tails
to power generators?

I want the job
of patting the dog
to keep its tail
wagging.

Dogs could generate
enough electricity
for cities, for countries—
light up the world!

Toothy Etiquette:
Chewing, Biting, and Fighting

Toothy activities are an integral part of loving and living with your dog. Dogs can easily be trained the appropriate chewy behavior. With a little patience, your pooch will teethe and chew with discerning taste.

Choosy Chewing

DO always leave your pooch in her crate with lots of chew toys stuffed with kibble, bones, and other goodies. While she is alone, she will entertain herself with good-tasting items that are vastly preferable to your bedroom slippers and couch pillows. She also will look forward to the crate or bed as a place to relax and chew herself to sleep. After you take her out of the crate and potty her, let her work on a stuffed Kong while you keep an eye on her.

DON'T ever leave your dog alone with a squeaky toy. These can be chewed up and swallowed.

By the time your dog is four and half months old, her adult teeth will be coming in and can be very destructive if not dealt with. So remember: If you leave her loose with nothing appropriate to chew on, you have only yourself to blame when she takes her boredom out on your closet, papers, and anything else within reach!

BEHAVIOR

Consider having your dog get all her food from stuffable chew toys or from you instead of a bowl. She will have to expend energy to get her food, which is natural, and it will keep her busy. Trainers call this a NILIF (nothing in life is free).

Soften the Bite: Appropriate Roughhousing

DO take the time out to get down on the floor and gently "playfight" with your pup. If he bites too hard, immediately let loose with a loud, high-pitched OWW! and walk away. Ignore the offending pooch for a minute before resuming play. Your dog should naturally learn not to hurt humans or other pets. Invite friends, children, and other dogs to meet your pooch. The more strangers your pup meets, the better. Teach your dog to tolerate being touched and handled by strangers. Make this a pleasant encounter by having friends offer treats. If your dog is calm and relaxed around them, let them roughhouse gently. Grab him softly by the collar, give him a treat, and continue playing. This way, your pooch learns that being taken by the collar is a good thing.

If your dog "fights" with other dogs but has learned not to bite down hard, he is very unlikely to cause injury.

Consult a trainer if your dog continues to snap, or if you suspect the dog you've adopted has been previously abused; bite moderation is very important.

DON'T hit the dog for biting; it will only teach him to bite—and fight—harder.

113

Roy: From Rags to Riches

by James Herriot

I had never before been deliberately on the lookout for Mrs. Donovan: she had just cropped up wherever I happened to be, but now I scanned the streets of Darrowby anxiously day by day without seeing her. I didn't like it when Gobber Newhouse got drunk and drove his bicycle determinedly through a barrier into a ten-foot hole where they were laying the new sewer and Mrs. Donovan was not in evidence among the happy crowd who watched the council workmen and two policemen trying to get him out; and when she was nowhere to be seen when they had to fetch the fire engine to the fish and chip shop the night the fat burst into flames, I became seriously worried.

Maybe I should have called round to see how she was getting on with that dog. Certainly I had trimmed off the dead tissue and dressed the sores before she took him away, but perhaps he needed something more than that. And yet at the time I had felt a strong conviction that the main thing was to get him out of there and clean him and feed him and nature would do the rest. And I had a lot of faith in Mrs. Donovan—far more than she had in me—when it came to animal doctoring; it was hard to believe I'd been completely wrong.

Roy

It must have been nearly three weeks and I was on the point of calling her at home when I noticed her stumping briskly along the far side of the marketplace, peering closely into every shop window exactly as before. The only difference was that she had a big yellow dog on the end of the lead.

I turned the wheel and sent my car bumping over the cobbles till I was abreast of her. When she saw me getting out she stopped and smiled impishly but she didn't speak as I bent over Roy and examined him. He was still a skinny dog but he looked bright and happy, his wounds were healing healthily, and there was not a speck of dirt in his coat or on his skin. I knew then what Mrs. Donovan had been doing all this time; she had been washing and combing and teasing at that filthy tangle until she finally conquered it.

As I straightened up she seized my wrist in a grip of surprising strength and looked up into my eyes.

"Now, Mr. Herriot," she said, "haven't I made a difference to this dog!"

"You've done wonders, Mrs. Donovan," I said. "And you've been at him with that marvelous shampoo of yours, haven't you?"

She giggled and walked away and from that day I saw the two of them frequently but at a distance and something like two months went by before I had a chance to talk to her again. She was passing by the surgery as I was coming down the steps and again she grabbed my wrist.

"Mr. Herriot," she said, just as she had done before, "haven't I made a difference to this dog!"

I looked down at Roy with something akin to awe. He had grown and filled out and his coat, no longer yellow but a rich gold, lay in luxuriant shining swathes over the well-fleshed ribs and back. A new, brightly studded collar glittered on his neck and his tail, beautifully fringed fanned the air gently. He was now a golden retriever in full magnificence. As I stared at him he reared up, plunked his forepaws on my chest, and looked into my face, and in his eyes I read plainly the same calm affection and trust I had seen back in that black, noisome shed.

"Mrs. Donovan," I said softly, he's the most beautiful dog in Yorkshire." Then, because I knew she was waiting for it, "It's those wonderful condition powders. Whatever do you put in them?"

"Why, wouldn't you like to know!" She bridled and smiled up at me coquettishly and indeed she was nearer being kissed at that moment than for many years.

~

I suppose you could say that was the start of Roy's second life. And as the years passed I often pondered on the beneficent providence which had decreed that an animal which had spent his first twelve months abandoned and unwanted, staring uncomprehendingly into that unchanging

R o y

stinking darkness, should be whisked in a moment into an
existence of light and movement and love. Because I don't
think any dog had it quite so good as Roy from then on.

His diet changed dramatically from odd bread crusts to best
stewing steak and biscuit, meaty bones and a bowl of warm
milk every evening. And he never missed a thing. Garden
fetes, school sports, gymkhanas—he'd be there. I was pleased
to note that as time went on Mrs. Donovan seemed to be
clocking up an even greater daily mileage. Her expenditure
on shoe leather must have been phenomenal, but of course
it was absolute pie for Roy—a busy round in the morning,
home for a meal then straight out again; it was all go.

Mrs. Donovan didn't confine her activities to the town
center; there was a big stretch of common land down by the
river where there were seats, and people used to take their
dogs for a gallop and she liked to get down there fairly regularly to check on the latest developments on the domestic
scene. I often saw Roy loping majestically over the grass
among a pack of assorted canines, and when he wasn't
doing that he was submitting to being stroked or patted or
generally fussed over. He was handsome and he just liked
people; it made him irresistible.

It was common knowledge that his mistress had bought a
whole selection of brushes and combs of various sizes with
which she labored over his coat. Some people said she had a
little brush for his teeth, too, and it might have been true,

but he certainly wouldn't need his nails clipped—his life on the roads would keep them down.

Mrs. Donovan, too, had her reward; she had a faithful companion by her side every hour of the day and night. But there was more to it than that; she had always had the compulsion to help and heal animals and the salvation of Roy was the high point of her life—a blazing triumph which never dimmed.

I know the memory of it was always fresh because many years later I was sitting on the sidelines at a cricket match and I saw the two of them; the old lady glancing keenly around her, Roy gazing placidly out at the field of play, apparently enjoying every ball. At the end of the match I watched them move away with the dispersing crowd; Roy would be about twelve then and heaven only knows how old Mrs. Donovan must have been, but the big golden animal was trotting along effortlessly and his mistress, a little more bent, perhaps, and her head rather nearer the ground, was going very well.

When she saw me she came over and I felt the familiar tight grip on my wrist.

"Mr. Herriot," she said, and in her eyes the pride was still as warm, the triumph still as bursting new as if it had all happened yesterday.

"Mr. Herriot, haven't I made a difference to this dog!" 🐾

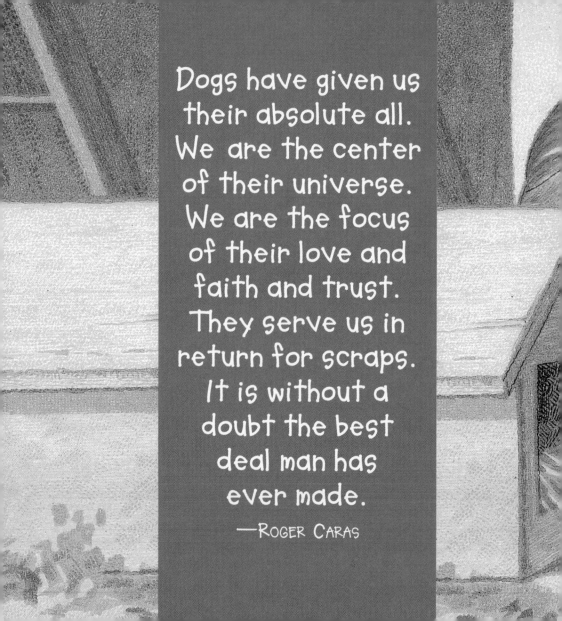

Dogs have given us
their absolute all.
We are the center
of their universe.
We are the focus
of their love and
faith and trust.
They serve us in
return for scraps.
It is without a
doubt the best
deal man has
ever made.

—ROGER CARAS

Hachiko: True Loyalty

Few animals could inspire an entire nation and the world to great admiration, but that is exactly what the legendary Akita dog Hachiko did. In 1924, Tokyo University professor Dr. Eisaburo Ueno acquired Hachiko, and the two lived in Ueno's home in Shibuya district of Tokyo. Each morning, Hachiko would accompany the professor to the train station for his morning commute and meet the professor in the afternoon for the walk home together. On May 21, 1925, when Hachiko was 18 months old, the professor failed to arrive at the train station. Sadly, he had suffered a stroke at the university and died. Nevertheless, Hachiko walked to the train station to meet the professor that afternoon as well as every morning and afternoon for the next 10 years—until Hachiko followed his master in death, passing away on the very spot at which he had last seen the professor. Today, Hachiko's image symbolizes tremendous loyalty and suffuses Japanese society—in the form of a bronze at the Shibuya train station, on the stage, on screen, in literature, and throughout Japanese folk culture. 🐾

Eve the Protector

Kathie Vaughn learned through a trying experience to trust the heightened senses and strength of her loyal canine companion, Eve, a 104-pound rottweiler. Minutes into a nightlong drive to an antiques show, Vaughn, who is paralyzed from the waist down, lost control of her customized van after an explosion erupted within the van's motor. Vaughn regained her ability to steer the smoking vehicle, thrust the passenger door open, and ordered Eve out of the inferno. Vaughn fumbled to reassemble her wheelchair, but Eve lunged into the van and gripped Vaughn's arm. Vaughn pulled away, trying to thwart Eve's efforts for fear of the dog's safety. But Eve seized her mistress by the leg this time and pulled her out and away from the van just as Vaughn blacked out. Vaughn regained consciousness in time to witness a tremendous explosion, with flames towering high into the night sky. Sensing the danger, Eve dragged Vaughn another 20 feet away from the blaze. When the authorities arrived, at first the loyal canine, in keeping with her protect instinct, would not let them approach her beloved Vaughn. 🐾

Verse for A Certain Dog

by Dorothy Parker

Such glorious faith as fills your limpid eyes,
  Dear little friend of mine, I never knew.
All-innocent are you, and yet all-wise.
  (For Heaven's sake, stop worrying that shoe!)
You look about, and all you see is fair;
  This mighty globe was made for you alone.
Of all the thunderous ages, you're the heir.
  (Get off the pillow with that dirty bone!)

A skeptic world you face with steady gaze;
    High in young pride you hold your noble head;
Gayly you meet the rush of roaring days.
    (Must you eat puppy biscuit on the bed?)
Lancelike your courage, gleaming swift and strong,
    Yours the white rapture of a wingèd soul,
Yours is a spirit like a May-day song.
    (God help you, if you break the goldfish bowl!)

"Whatever is, is good"—your gracious creed.
    You wear your joy of living like a crown.
Love lights your simplest act, your every deed.
    (Drop it, I tell you—put that kitten down!)
You are God's kindliest gift of all—a friend.
    Your shining loyalty unflecked by doubt,
You ask but leave to follow to the end.
    (Couldn't you wait until I took you out?)

This recipe is for traditional dog-bone cookies, but try using dog-themed cookie cutters that include a fire hydrant, paw print, doghouse, and bones. Check out www.cookiecutter.com.

For cookies:
1 egg
$1/2$ cup powdered milk
$1^1/_2$ teaspoons fresh parsley, very finely chopped
6 tablespoons olive oil
2 teaspoons honey
1 small jar beef or chicken baby food
$1/2$ cup low-sodium beef or chicken broth
$3/_4$ to $1^1/_4$ cups whole wheat flour
1/2 cup rye flour
1/2 cup rice flour
1/2 cup cracked wheat

For glaze:
1 egg
2 tablespoons chicken or beef broth or 1 tablespoon milk

1. Preheat oven to 350°F.

2. In a large bowl, com-bine all cookie ingredients but the flours and cracked wheat. Blend well.

3. Gradually mix in the flours and cracked wheat. Add enough wheat flour until the dough is stiff.

4. Place the dough on rolling surface and knead 3–5 minutes. Form into a ball and roll it out to $1/2$-inch thickness. Cut out cookies, gathering and using leftover pieces.

5. Place cookies on ungreased baking sheets and bake for 30 minutes.

6. Whisk egg and liquid together to make the glaze.

7. Apply glaze, turn, reglaze, and bake for another 30 minutes.

8. Cool. Refrigerate in air-tight container for up to 1 week, or freeze indefinitely.

Makes up to several dozen treats

Glazed Bones

Crimes Against Dog

by Alice Walker

Marley was an amazing comfort to me. What is it about dogs? I think what I most appreciate in Marley is how swiftly she forgives me. Anything. Was I cool and snooty when I got up this morning? Did I neglect to greet her when I came in from a disturbing movie? Was I a little short on the foodstuffs and did I forget to give her a cube of dried liver? Well. And what about that walk we didn't do and the swim we didn't take and why don't I play ball with her the way I did all last week? And who is this strange person you want me to go off with? It doesn't matter what it is, what crime against Dog I have committed, she always forgives me. She doesn't even appear to think about it. One minute she's noting my odd behavior, the next, if I make a move toward her, she's licking my hand. As if to say, Gosh, I'm so glad you're yourself again, and you're back!

Dogs understand something I was late learning: When we are mean to anyone or any being it is because we are temporarily not ourselves. We're somebody else inhabiting these bodies we think of as us. They recognize this. Ooops, I imagine Marley saying to herself, sniffing my anger, disap-

pointment, or distraction. My mommy's not in there at the moment. I'll just wait until she gets back. I've begun to feel this way more than a little myself. Which is to say, Marley is teaching me how to be more self-forgiving. Sometimes I will say something that hurts a friend's feelings. I will be miserable and almost want to do away with myself. Then I'll think, But that wasn't really the you that protects and loves this friend so much you would never hurt them. That was a you that slipped in because you are sad and depressed about other things: the state of your love life, your health, or the fate of the planet. The you that loves your friend is back now. Welcome her home. Be gentle with her. Tell her you understand. Lick her hand. 🐾

To err is human,
to forgive, canine.

—Anonymous

You Know You Are a Dog Person When . . .

- You have baby gates permanently installed at strategic places around the house, but no babies.

- You can't see out the passenger side of the windshield because there are nose–prints all over the inside.

- You have thirty–two different names for your dog. Most make no sense, but he or she understands.

- You like people who like your dog. You despise people who don't.

- You sign and send birthday, anniversary, and Christmas cards from your dog.

- You'd rather stay home on Saturday night and cuddle your dog than go to the movies with your sweetie.

- You shovel a zigzag path in the backyard snow so your dog can reach all his or her favorite spots.

- You avoid vacuuming the house as long as possible because your dog is afraid of the vacuum cleaner.

- Your parents refer to your pet as their granddog.

- You match your furniture, carpet, and clothes to your dog.

- You keep eating even after finding a dog hair in your pasta.

- Your license plate or license plate frame mentions your dog.

- You don't go to happy hours with coworkers anymore because you need to go home and see your dog.

- Your dog sees the vet, while you settle for an over-the-counter remedy from the drugstore.

- You don't give a second thought to using the dog's brush to give a quick run-through on your own hair.

- You cringe at the price of food in the grocery store but think nothing of the cost of dog food or treats.

- You pick up your latest roll of film and there isn't a single picture of a two-legged person in it...

- You carry pictures of your dog in your wallet instead of pictures of your parents, significant other, or anyone human.

The neighbors' dog will not stop barking.
He *is* barking the *same* high, rhythmic bark
that he barks every time they leave the house.
They must switch him on on their way out.

The neighbors' dog will not stop barking.
I close all the windows in the house
and put on a Beethoven symphony full blast
but I can still hear him muffled under the music,
barking, barking, barking,

and now I can see him sitting in the orchestra,
his head raised confidently as if Beethoven
had included a part for barking dog.

When the record finally ends he is still barking,
sitting there in the oboe section barking,
his eyes fixed on the conductor who is
entreating him with his baton

while the other musicians listen in respectful
silence to the famous barking dog solo,
that endless coda that first established
Beethoven as an innovative genius.

Another Reason Why I Don't Keep a Gun in The House

by Billy Collins

MOUTH OPEN, tongue hanging limply, soft droopy eyes, ears forward—"I'm chillin'." (relaxed attitude)

GLANCING SIDEWAYS or away with wide-open eyes, flattened ears, jaws clenched or tongue licking lips, panting, tail tucked under—"I'm scared." (anxiety or fearfulness)

Dogspeak

Two dogs meeting for the first time can size each other up without even a bark or a growl. In a matter of moments, with a series of glances and postures, they know whether they're going to be buddies or enemies.

TEETH BARED, eyes staring, ears flattened forward, tail horizontal and wagging slowly, a low growl that originates in the chest and progresses to a snarl—"Come closer and I might bite." (intimidation tactic)

YAWNING—"I need some alone time." (stress)

HEAD DOWN or turned to side—"You're the boss." (submissive gesture)

HEAD HIGH, tail up, body tensed and still—"Hey, what's that?" or "Sure, look me over over. I'll bet I can outrun you!" (conveys interest, or a challenge to another dog)

A LOW, assertive growl—"Get off my property!" (territoriality)

HEAD OR PAWS RESTING on another dog–"I'm the boss of you." (dominant gesture)

HEAD LOW, rump in the air, a light, high-pitched bark or soft play-growling– "C'mon, let's party! I've got the ball, see if you can take it from me!" (an invitation or playful challenge)

RAISING OF HAIRS along neck and/or back–"I'm ready to fight you." (threat posture)

TURNING AND HOPPING, with short, high-pitched yips or a happy howl–"Hi! It's good to see you!" (excitement)

LOUD, repeated barking, sometimes with a growl– "Get away or I'll bite you!" (aggression)

SHORT, sharp barks or a low whine–"Danger!" or "Something's out there!" (alert)

LOW, moaning barking, with a low, whining growl "Who's out there?" (worry or anxiety)

ROLLING OVER, showing belly–"Don't hurt me, Boss." (deference posture)

LOOMING over another dog, tail wagging–"Because I said so." (dominant posture)

LONG, sustained howling–"Why did you leave me out here alone?" (separation anxiety)

A SCREAMING WHINE–"Uncle!" (when being beaten in a fight by a dominant dog) or "Stop! It hurts!"

The Soul of A Dog

by Daniel Pinkwater

Once, Jill had fun with our Alaskan malamute, Arnold, by pretending that she was teaching him a nursery song. It was pure nonsense—Jill was tending our old-fashioned, nonautomatic clothes washer, and Arnold was keeping her company.

Jill sang him the song about the eensy beensy spider, and indicated where he was supposed to join in. He did so, with something between a scream of anguish and the call of a moose in rut.

The next time she had laundry to do, Arnold appeared, and sat squirming excitedly until she sang him the song. He came in on cue. Arnold learned a number of songs. His vocal range was limited, but his ear was good.

It was also Arnold who taught Juno, our other dog, to set up a howl whenever we passed a McDonald's. On a vacation trip, we'd breakfasted on Egg McMuffins for a week, and the dogs always got an English muffin. They never forgot.

I once observed Arnold taking care of an eight-week-old kitten. The kitten was in a cage. Arnold wanted to go and sleep in his private corner, but every time the kitten cried, he'd drag himself to his feet, slouch over to the cage and lie

down with his nose between the wires, so the kitten could sink its tiny claws into it. When the kitten became quiet, Arnold would head for his corner and flop, exhausted. Immediately the kitten would cry, and Arnold would haul himself back to the cage. I counted this performance repeated over forty times.

Arnold acquired friends. People would visit him.

My friend Don Yee would borrow Arnold sometimes, and they'd drive to the White Castle and eat hamburgers.

He was the sort of dog you could talk things over with. 🐾

Obsessive Activities

Your hound has turned howling into an Olympic event. Your shepherd mix is going to scratch right through your basement door, and your terrier is excavating a tunnel big enough for a subway in your backyard. Horrors! Don't reach for a stick to beat them with—read on.

Speak! Hush! Getting a Motor-Mouth under Control

DO teach your dog to speak, and when not to. If you can teach her to speak, you can teach her to hush. "Capture" this behavior the next time your pup barks or growls at the doorbell or some other noise by rewarding her with a treat. To make training fast and efficient, mark the bark with "Good!" or the sound of a dog clicker. Once she seems to be getting the hang of it, add the cue "Speak!" just before she barks. Do not reward her for speaking without the cue. She will learn to stop barking when she doesn't "get paid" for talking out of turn. Add the cue "Hush!" and give her a treat for quieting herself. Your dog will learn that when you are not giving the cue, she should not bark.

DON'T subject your dog to long-term confinement. Don't leave your dog outside in isolation; he will learn to bark and howl to relieve boredom and loneliness.

Digging and Scratching

DO invite your best four-legged friend into the house. The answer to this problem is the same as for howling and barking:

Housebreak and chew-train your dog, and you can bring her inside to live with you and give her the attention she deserves. Dogs are not solitary creatures. Dogs vocalize and do "yard work" out of boredom. Interact with your dog, and she will want to play Frisbee with you instead of digging.

DON'T reward your dog simply for not digging and expect her to understand which of the million things she didn't do today earned that treat. Some behaviorists call this a "dead man" behavior; the trainee has no idea what she did right and therefore doesn't learn anything.

A Conversation with My Dogs

by Merrill Markoe

It is late afternoon. Seated at my desk, I call for my dogs to join me in my office. They do.

Me: The reason I've summoned you here today is I really think we should talk about something.

Bob: What's that?

Me: Well, please don't take this the wrong way, but I get the feeling you guys think you *have* to follow me *everywhere* and I just want you both to know that you don't.

Stan: Where would you get a feeling like that?

Me: I get if from the fact that the both of you follow me *everywhere* all day long. Like for instance, this morning. We were all together in the bedroom? Why do you both look blank? Doesn't this ring a bell at all? I was on the bed reading the paper . . .

Bob: Where was I?

Me: On the floor sleeping.

Bob: On the floor sleepi . . . ? Oh, yes. Right. I remember that. Go on.

Me: So, there came a point where I had to get up and go

into the next room to get a Kleenex. And you *both* woke up out of a deep sleep to go with me.

Stan: Yes. So? What's the problem?

Bob: We *like* to watch you get Kleenex. We happen to think it's something you do very well.

Me: The point I'm trying to make is why do you both have to get up out of a deep sleep to go *with* me. You sit there staring at me, all excited, like you think something really good is going to happen. I feel a lot of pressure to be more entertaining.

Bob: Would it help if we stood?

Stan: I think what the lady is saying is that where Kleenex retrieval is concerned, she'd just as soon we not make the trip.

Bob: Is that true?

Me: Yes. It is.

Bob (*deeply hurt*): Oh, man.

Stan: Don't let her get to you, buddy.

Bob: I know I shouldn't. But it all comes as such a shock.

Me: I think you may be taking this wrong. It's not that I don't like your company. It's just that I see no reason for you both to follow me every time I get up.

Bob: What if just one of us goes?

Stan: And I don't suppose that "one of us" would be you?"

Me: *Neither* of you needs to go.

Bob: Okay. Fine. No problem. Get your damn Kleenex alone from now on.

Me: Good.

Bob: I'm just curious. What's your position on pens?

Me: Pens?

Bob: Yes. How many of us can wake up out of a deep sleep to watch you look for a pen?

Me: Why would *either* of you want to wake up out of a deep sleep to follow me around while I'm looking for a pen?

Stan: Is she serious?

Bob: I can't tell. She has such a weird sense of humor.

Me: Let's just level with each other, okay? The *real* reason you both follow me every place I go is that you secretly believe there might be food involved. Isn't that true? Isn't that the real reason for the show of enthusiasm?

Stan: Very nice talk.

Bob: The woman has got some mouth on her.

Me: You mean you *deny* that every time you follow me out of the room it's actually because you think we're stopping for snacks?

Bob: Absolutely false. That is a bald-faced lie. We do it for the life experience. Period.

Stan: And sometimes I think it might work into a game of ball.

Bob: But we certainly don't *expect* anything.

Stan: We're way past expecting anything of you. We wouldn't want you to overexert yourself in any way. You have to rest and save up all your strength for all that Kleenex fetching.

Bob: Plus we know it doesn't concern you in the least that we're both *starving to death*.

Stan: We consume on the average about a third of the calories eaten daily by the typical wasted South American street dog.

Me: *One* bowl of food a day is what the *vet* said I should give you. No more.

Bob: One bowl of food is a joke. It's an hors d'oeuvre. It does nothing but whet my appetite.

Me: Last summer, before I cut your food down, you were the size and shape of a hassock.

Bob: Who is she talking to?

Stan: You, pal. You looked like a beanbag chair, buddy.

Bob: But it was not from overeating. IN summer, I retain fluids, that's all. I was in very good shape.

Stan: For a hippo. I saw you play ball back then. Nice energy. For a dead guy.

Bob: Don't talk to me about energy. Who single-handedly

147

ate his way through the back fence. Not just once but on *four separate occasions*?

Me: So *you're* the one who did that?

Bob: One who did what?

Me: Ate through the back fence.

Bob: Is there something wrong with the back fence? I have no idea what happened. Whoever said that is a liar.

Stan: The fact remains that we are starving all day long and you continually torture us by eating right in front of us.

Bob: Very nice manners, by the way.

Me: You have the nerve to discuss my manners? Who drinks out of the toilet and then comes up and kisses me on the face?

Bob: That would be Dave.

Me: No. That would be *you*. And while we're on the subject of manners, who keeps trying to crawl *into* the refrigerator? Who always has *mud* on their tongue?

Stan: Well, that would be Dave.

Me: Okay. That *would* be Dave. But the point I'm trying to make is that where manners are concerned, let's just say that you don't catch me trying to stick my head in *your* dinner.

Bob: Well, that may be more a function of menu than anything else.

Me: Which brings me right back to my original point. The

two of you do not have to wake up and offer me fake camaraderie now that you understand that *once* a day is all you're ever going to be fed. Period. Nonnegotiable. For the rest of your natural lives. And if I want to play ball, I'll *say so*. End of sentence.

Stan: Well, I see that the nature of these talks has completely broken down.

Bob: I gotta tell you, it hurts.

Me: There's no reason to have hurt feelings.

Stan: Fine. Whatever you say.

Bob: I just don't give a damn anymore. I'm beyond that, quite frankly. Get your own Kleenex, for all I care.

Stan: I feel the same way. Let her go get all the Kleenex and pens she wants. I couldn't care less.

Me: Excellent. Well, I hope we understand each other now.

Bob: We do. Why'd you get up? Where are you going?

Me: Into the next room.

Stan: Oh. Mm hmm. I see. And why is that?

Me: To get my purse.

Stan: Hey, fatso, out of my way.

Bob: Watch out, #@*%$, I was first.

Stan: The hell you were *I* was first.

Bob: #@%*$. We're getting her purse, I go first. I'm *starving*.

Stan: You don't listen at all, do you? Going for *pens* means food. She said she's getting her *purse*. That means *ball*. 🐾

I've seen a look in dogs' eyes, a quickly vanishing look of amazed contempt, and I am convinced that basically dogs think humans are nuts.

—JOHN STEINBECK

Presidential Dogs ★ ★ ★ ★ ★ ★

Many species of animals have called the White House home, from cats, birds, rodents, and rabbits, to horses, cows, mules, and even elephants. Yet dogs have always held the most prominent positions of any presidential pet since the very genesis of the United States. Twenty-nine out of forty-three presidents were dog-owners. American presidents have owned more than one hundred dogs total. Here are some fun facts of the loveable canines that have provided fodder for both national scandals and heartwarming comic relief.

★ JOHN F. KENNEDY owned at least ten dogs during his presidency, more than any other American president.

★ GEORGE H. W. BUSH's springer spaniel, Millie, was the subject of a book that sold more copies than the autobiography of the president himself.

★ RONALD REAGAN's Bouvier des Flandres, Lucky, was photographed dragging the president across the White House lawn in the presence of Margaret Thatcher, and later sent to live in California due to the national embarrassment.

★ GERALD FORD's golden retriever, Lucky, gave birth to nine puppies at the White House.

★ ★ ★ ★ ★ ★ ★ ★ ★ ★ ★ ★ ★ ★ ★ ★ ★ ★ ★ ★

★ **LYNDON B. JOHNSON** always shook hands with his white collie, Blanco, whenever he left or returned to the White House.

★ **JOHN F. KENNEDY**'s Welsh terrier, Pushinka, was the offspring of the Russian space dog Strelka and a gift of the Russian premier Krushchev.

★ **FRANKLIN DELANO ROOSEVELT**'s Scottish terrier, Fala, was the star of an MGM Hollywood movie about the typical day of a dog in the White House. Fala is also depicted in the Franklin Delano Roosevelt Memorial. His other Scottish terrier, Meggie, became infamous for biting a senator.

★ **WARREN HARDING**'s Airedale, Laddie Boy, had his own chair to sit on at Cabinet meetings.

★ **THEODORE ROOSEVELT**'s bull terrier, Pete, tore off the French ambassador's pants during a White House function, nearly causing an international scandal.

Activities for Groups

Nothing goes better with dogs than kids, whether age 6 or 60. And little else provides for better photo ops. These activities can really bring out your pooch's personality, and her abilities may astonish you.

THE RECALL GAME Give everyone several pieces of kibble and have them sit in a circle with your puppy in the middle. Players take turns rapping twice on the floor and treating the dog when she comes. Challenge the pup to run back and forth at random, not to the next person in the circle. As the game progresses, have players say the pup's name and "Come!" as they rap. An advanced version of this game is Puppy Push-Ups (p. 303).

DOGGY CIRCUS Use dog agility course ideas (p. 97) to set up a backyard circus, complete with pedestals for your "wild" animals. If your dog does a reliable sit, try teaching her to "sit pretty" for a beauty contest. Raising a treat high over a sitting dog's head will usually prompt her to sit up. Once she masters that, substitute a stick, or "baton," for the lure. From sitting pretty, it's just a hop, skip, and, er, twirl to doggie dancing! Give prizes for dogs who stay up longest, do the fastest twirl, and hurdle the highest.

BIRTHDAY PARTY Help your kids celebrate their dog's birthday in style. Bake your pooch a cake, using the Bake a Cake kit, available at various online retailers. This canine confection comes in either a liver- or oatmeal-flavored mix, complete with a beautifully decorated bone-shaped cake tin. Take pictures for your scrapbook—and while you're at it, the humans can play a round of Dogopoly, "The Game of High Steaks and Bones," available at various retailers.

FAMILY TREE Dogs, wolves, and foxes are descended from a small, tree-dwelling, weasel-like mammal that existed about 40 million years ago.

SOUND THE ALERT A dog can smell chemical changes in the air, often including those that occur when its owner is ill or about to have a seizure, even when the person is completely unaware of it. For this reason, many people now use service dogs as seizure-alert dogs.

Doggy Data

SIZE MATTERS The Irish wolfhound ranks generally as the largest breed, the Chihuahua is the smallest dog, and the Saint Bernard is generally the heaviest. Giving the Chihuahua breed a run for its money, one Yorkshire terrier weighed in at only 283.5 grams, about ten ounces.

SEE ME, SMELL ME A dog senses objects first by their movement, second by their brightness, and third by their shape. Dogs, whose vision is not as acute as humans', are considered somewhat color-blind. Their noses, however, are 1000 times better than ours.

TOP DOG According to the American Kennel Club, the Labrador retriever has dominated its list of registered canines for 12 years straight. The number of registered Labs is nearly three times the number of golden retrievers, the dog in the number-two spot.

ANATOMY LESSON A dog's heart beats from 70 to 120 times a minute, while the human heart beats 70 to 80 times a minute. Dogs and humans are the only animals with prostates.

DREAM ON Healthy puppies whimper, roll their eyes, and twitch vigorously while sleeping. This dreaming is normal, and aids in nervous-system development.

BIGGEST ON THE BLOCK The heaviest and longest dog on record was an Old English mastiff named Zorba. In 1989, Zorba weighed in at 343 pounds, and measured 8 feet, 3 inches long from nose to tail!

MODEL TYPES Tallest among the breeds are the great dane and Irish wolfhound.

HEAR, HEAR! Dogs can hear sounds 250 yards away that are undetectable by the human ear beyond 25 yards. Canine ears detects sound waves that vibrate at frequencies of more than 30,000 times a second, while we can hear frequencies of only up to 20,000 times a second, and cats, 25,000.

157

Travels with Charley

by John Steinbeck

In 1960, when he was almost 60 years old, John Steinbeck set out to rediscover his native land. Accompanied only by a French poodle named Charley, he traveled the length and the breadth of the United States.

And I sat in the seat and faced what I had concealed from myself. I was driving myself, pounding out the miles because I was no longer hearing or seeing. I had passed my limit of taking in or, like a man who goes on stuffing in food after he is filled, I felt helpless to assimilate what was fed in through my eyes. Each hill looked like the one just passed. I have felt this way in the Prado in Madrid after looking at a hundred paintings—the stuffed and helpless inability to see more.

This would be a time to find a sheltered place beside a stream to rest and refurbish. Charley, in the dark seat beside me, mentioned a difficulty with a little moaning sigh. I had even forgotten him. I let him out and he staggered to the hill of broken bottles, sniffed at them, and took another way.

The night air was very cold, shivery cold, so that I lighted the cabin and turned up the gas to warm the air. The cabin was not neat. My bed was unmade and breakfast dishes lay desolate in the sink. I sat on the bed and stared into gray

dreariness. Why had I though I could learn anything about
the land? For the last hundreds of miles I had avoided people.
Even at necessary stops for gasoline I had answered in
monosyllables and retained no picture. My eye and brain
had welshed on me. I was fooling myself that this was
important or even instructive. There was a ready remedy, of
course. I reached out the whisky bottle without getting up,
poured half a tumbler, smelled it, and poured it back in the
bottle. No remedy was there.

Charley had not returned. I opened the door and whistled
him and got no response. That shook me out of it. I grabbed
my searchlight and turned its spearing beam up the
canyon. The light flashed on two eyes about fifty
yards away. I ran up the trail and found him
standing staring into space, just as I had been.

"What's the matter, Charley, aren't you well?"
His tail slowly waved his replies.
"Oh, yes. Quite well, I guess."
"Why didn't you come when I whistled?"
"I didn't hear you whistle."
"What are you staring at?"
"I don't know. Nothing I guess."
"Well, don't you want your dinner?"
"I'm really not hungry. But I'll go through the motions."
Back in the cabin he flopped down on the floor and put
his chin down on his paws.

"Come on up on the bed, Charley. Let's be miserable together." He complied but without enthusiasm and I riffled my fingers in his topknot and behind his ears the way he likes it. "How's that?"

He shifted his head. "A little more to the left. There. That's the place."

"We'd be lousy explorers. A few days out and we get the mullygrubs. The first white man through here—I think he was named Narváez and I'm under the impression his little jaunt took six years. Move over. I'll look it up. Nope, it was eight years—1528 to 1536. And Narváez himself didn't make it this far. Four of his men did, though. I wonder if they ever got the mullygrubs. We're soft, Charley. Maybe it's time for a little gallantry. When's your birthday?"

"I don't know. Maybe it's like horses, the first of January."

"Think it might be today?"

"Who knows?"

"I could make you a cake. Have to be hotcake mix because that's what I have. Plenty of syrup and a candle on top."

Charley watched the operation with some interest. His silly tail made delicate conversation. "Anybody saw you make a birthday cake for a dog that he don't even know when's his birthday would think you were nuts."

"If you can't manage any better grammar than that with your tail, maybe it's a good thing you can't talk."

It turned out pretty well—four layers of hotcakes with maple syrup between and a stub of a miner's candle on top. I drank Charley's health in straight whisky as he ate and licked up the syrup. And then we both felt better. But there was Narváez' party—eight years. There were men in those days.

Charley licked the syrup from his whiskers. "What makes you so moony?"

"It's because I've stopped seeing. When that happens you think you'll never see again."

He stood up and stretched himself, first fore and then aft. "Let's take a stroll up the hill," he suggested. "Maybe you've started again."

We inspected the pile of broken whisky bottles and then continued up the trail. The dry, frozen air came out of us in plumes of steam. Some fairly large animal went leaping up the broken stone hill, or maybe a small animal and a big little avalanche.

"What does your nose say that was?"

"Nothing I recognize. Kind of a musky smell. Nothing I'm going to chase, either."

So dark was the night that it was prickled with fiery dots. My light brought an answering flash up the steep rocky bank. I climbed up, slipping and floundering, lost the echoed light and found it again, a good little new-split stone with a piece of mica in it—not a fortune but a good thing to have. I put it in my pocket and we went to bed.

NUX VOMICA.

How Many Dogs Does It Take to Change a Lightbulb?

Afghan: Lightbulb? What lightbulb?

Australian shepherd: Put all the bulbs in a little circle. . .

Beagle: Lightbulb? Lightbulb? That thing I ate was a lightbulb?

Border collie: Just one? I'll replace any wiring that's not up to code.

Chihuahua: We don't need no stinking lightbulb.

Cocker spaniel: Why change it? I can still pee on the carpet in the dark.

Dachshund: I can't reach the stupid lamp!

Doberman pinscher: While it's dark, I'm going to sleep on the couch.

German shepherd: I'll change it as soon as I've led these people from the dark, check to make sure I haven't missed any, and make just one more perimeter patrol to see that no one has tried to take advantage of the situation.

Canine Crackups

Greyhound: It isn't moving. Who cares?

Golden retriever: The sun is shining, the day is young, we've got our whole lives ahead of us, and you're inside worrying about a stupid burned-out lightbulb?

Hound dog: Zzzzzzzzzzzzzzzzzzzzzzzzzzz.

Irish wolfhound: Can somebody else do it? I've got a hangover.

Jack Russell terrier: I'll just pop it in while I'm bouncing off the walls.

Labrador: Oh, me, me!!!! Pleeeeeeze let me change the lightbulb!!! Can I? Can I? Huh? Huh? Can I?

Mastiff: Mastiffs are NOT afraid of the dark.

Malamute: Let the border collie do it. You can feed me while he's busy.

Old English sheep dog: Lightbulb? I'm sorry, but I don't see a lightbulb.

Pointer: I see it! There it is! Right there!

Rottweiller: Go Ahead! Make me!

Shih tzu: Puh-leeez, dahling. I have servants for that kind of thing.

Toy poodle: I'll just blow in the border collie's ear and he'll do it. By the time he finishes rewiring the house, my nails will be dry.

Search and Destroy

This activity provides mental stimulation as it gets progressively more challenging with each session. The secret is to keep it exciting while not progressing so fast that your dog loses interest. Eventually, you may be able to hide the toy in a far region of your house or property and have your pooch use her nose to find it. Perhaps you should do this with your car keys or TV remote! It's helpful if your dog already knows sit, or is willing to hold off and wait for a moment while you hide the object. If not, though, she will soon get the idea.

one willing pooch, one human partner, a favorite toy

1. Pick a toy your dog can really sink her teeth into: a ratty old sock with a ball in it, a rubber squeaky toy, etc. Show your pooch the toy (you might tease her with it to get her stirred up, but you probably won't need to).

2. Put the toy under a towel or behind a door and give the signal "Search!" or "Sic 'em!"

3. Get excited when your dog finds it. Let her work out her aggressions on it (this is her reward) before you ask her to give it up for another round.

4. As the dog catches on, hide the toy farther and farther away, and don't let her go after it until you give the cue. At first, leave a part of the toy exposed to make it easier to find.

Variation: Search and Eat. If your dog is advanced enough, have her do a sit-stay while you hide treats around the house.

Puppyproofing Your Home

He's a member of the family, and just like a toddler, your new puppy explores the world by putting things in his mouth. Your sweet, cuddly little friend's lack of common sense can get him into a ton of trouble if you don't take some important precautions. These are advisable for both little ones and full-grown pooches.

SCOUT FOR TOXINS. The bottle of antifreeze in your storeroom is particularly poisonous to your dog, as pets are attracted to its sweet flavor. Lock away all chemicals, cleaners, and medications. While you're at it, search your property for any toxic spills, rusting equipment, lead paint, small items that can be swallowed, and other hazards.

TAPE DOWN or cover electrical cords to prevent chewing and electrical shocks. Place poisonous plants out of reach. Some scented soaps and hygiene-product wrappings made from vegetable materials are attractive but hazardous appetizers to your dog.

MAKE SURE your garbage is tightly covered so that your dog can't get into it. Chicken and turkey bones, poisonous foods, and inedible objects scavenged from the trash are common reasons for a trip to the animal emergency room.

EXAMINE your baseboards and furniture for holes, jagged edges, loose pieces, and nails that might injure your pup.

HAVE ON HAND plenty of stain remover, odor neutralizer from the pet supply, and absorbent rags. Always supervise an uncrated pup. An accident should never happen, but if it does, immediately place an old towel or stack of newspapers under the rug and soak the spot with odor destroyer.

DON'T LEAVE squeaky toys and other small items that can be torn up and swallowed lying around. Many toys are meant to played with only under supervision.

COVER your cat's litter box to keep your pooch from, er, "sampling." Pups have some funny habits, and some will swallow just about anything!

PAY ATTENTION to the cleaners you use on the surfaces of your home, and rinse well. Dogs sometimes lick floors and other smooth surfaces.

Tread softly the floor is soaped

Joxer, bouncing harlequin,
All ingratiating grin,
Which begat thee, jolly Joxer?
Airedale, poodle, beagle, boxer?
Scottie braw or Irish terrier?
Never mind, the more the merrier;
A pedigree *so* heterodox
Perks up thy personality, Jox,
For thou, rambunctious residual,
Wert whelped unique and individual,
A blithe buffoon, a jester pampered,
Nor by the Ten Commandments hampered
(I know thou triflest with the Seventh),
But Joxer, mind the *stern* Eleventh,
Or learn from choking leash and baffling tether
Thy neighbor's Leghorns thou shalt not de-feather.

To A Foolish Dog

by Ogden Nash

The Dog Park

In its most general sense, "dog park" means a place where dogs can play off-leash. And play, they do! It can be enclosed or open, indoors, outdoors, huge, small, charge an entrance fee, require membership—or not. Some parks are exclusive clubs, or even doggy day-care facilities complete with swimming pools and caretakers who satisfy your dog's every whim. A dog park is a great neighborhood addition. Everyone enjoys watching the antics of dogs at play.

Starting and maintaining a dog park requires a committed dog-owner group to make sure everyone follows the rules. Find out what these are before going in. Most public parks will strictly enforce feces disposal. Some even provide pooper-scoop bags and other equipment by holding fund-raisers. The local dog-owner group may have rules that include health requirements before a dog is allowed in.

You would be well advised to make sure your pet's shots and preventive treatments are up to date. Distemper is a terrible disease, and you don't want to bring home a dog-load of fleas, either!

Before crossing that off-leash threshold, stand outside and observe the park. Is it clean? Are the owners attentive? Do the dogs seem to be well cared for? Are they calm, or is the park crowded and out of control? Does the group play too aggressively for your dog? Are there special hours for small dogs? Will owners let your dog meet their dogs on-leash before going in? Most well-socialized dogs play together without fighting because the park is a neutral territory, though altercations do arise. Watchful owners will distract and soothe dogs before a disagreement escalates to violence. Always take a pocketful of treats with you for this purpose.

Street Smarts: Stepping Out

*W*ho's walking whom, anyway? Remember, you are the master, and an obedient dog is a happy dog. But obedience should be safe and comfortable, and doesn't necessarily involve merely strolling with a leash!

DO train your dog to heel on cue (see Teaching the Heel, p. 294). For your dog's and others' safety, you won't always want to let her go trotting madly out in front of you, especially on a busy sidewalk. Do use a Gentle Leader Headcollar (available at www.gentleleader.com) or similar training collar and leash instead of a choker while training. This type of collar applies soft pressure to the back of the neck instead of the front. Since dogs fight and pull against pressure, the training collar signals them to slow up when you need them to, and quickly ends unwanted leash pulling.

Other times, you might want to encourage the dog to pull—it's fun! Vary heeling sessions with periods when you allow her full rein.

DON'T use an extendable leash on busy city sidewalks; you can't control your dog. This presents a tremendous hazard to other pedestrians, especially the elderly or disabled. If you do not exercise manners and caution, you can't expect your dog to!

The Thin Red Leash

by James Thurber

It takes courage for a tall thin man to lead a tiny Scotch terrier pup on a smart red leash in our neighborhood, that region bounded roughly (and how!) by Hudson and West Streets, where the Village takes off its Windsor tie and dons its stevedore corduroys. Here men and guys and all dogs are part bull. Here 'cute' apartments stand quivering like pioneers on the prairie edge.

The first day that I sallied forth with Black Watch III bounding tinily at the street end of the thin red leash, a cement finisher, one of the crowd that finds an esoteric pleasure in standing on the bleak corner of Hudson and Horatio Streets, sat down on the sidewalk and guffawed. There were hoots and whistles.

It was apparent that the staunch and plucky Scotch terrier breed was, to these uninitiated bulldog-lovers, the same as Pekingese. But Black Watch must have his airing. So I continued to brave such witticisms as "Hey, fella, where's the rest of it?" and—this from a huge steamfitter—"What d'y say me an' you an' the dog go somewheres and have tea?"

Once a dockworker demanded, in a tone indicating he would not take Black Watch III for an answer, "What's that thing's name?"

My courage failed me. "Mike," I said, giving the leash a red-blooded jerk and cursing the Scotty. The whole affair was a challenge to my gumption. I had been scared to call my dog by its right name.

The gang was on hand in full force the next evening. One of them snapped enormous calloused fingers at Black Watch and he bounded away, leash and all, from my grasp.

"Black Watch!" I shouted—if you could call it shouting.

"What did y' call that dog, fella?" demanded a man who, I think blows through truck exhaust whistles to test them.

"Black Watch," said I.

"What's that mean?" he asked menacingly.

"It was a Scottish regiment wiped out at Ypres or somewhere." I said, pronouncing it 'Eeprr.'

"Wiped out where?" he snarled.

"Wiped out at Wipers," I said.

"That's better," he said.

I again realized that I had shown the white feather. That night I took a solemn, if not fervent, oath to tell the next heavy-footed lout that flayed my dog to go to hell. The following evening the gang was more numerous than ever. A gigantic chap lunged forward at us. He had the build of a smokestack-wrecker.

"Psst!" he hissed. Black Watch held his ground.

"They're scrappers, these dogs," I protested amiable.

"What d' they scrap—cockroaches?" asked another man, amid general laughter. I realized that now was the time to die. After all there are certain slurs that you can't take about your dog—gang or no gang. Just then a monstrous man, evidently a former Hudson Duster who lifts locomotives from track to track when the turn tables are out of order, lounged out of a doorway.

"Whadda we got here?" he growled.

"Park Avenoo pooch," sneered one gas-house gangster. The train lifter eyed Black Watch, who was wagging his tail in a most friendly manner.

"Scotty, ain't it?" asked the train-lifter, producing a sack of scrap tobacco.

"Yeah," I said, as easily as I could.

"Damn fine dogs, Scotties," said the train-lifter. "You gotta good 'un there, when it puts on some age, scout. Hellcats in a fight, too, I mean. Seen one take the tonsils out of a Airedale one day."

"Yeah?" asked the smokestack-wrecker.

"Yeah," said the train-lifter.

"Yeah," said I.

Several huge hands went down to pat a delighted shaggy head. There were no more catcalls or hoots. Black Watch III had been acquitted of Pomeranianism. We're quite good friends now, Black Watch and the gang and I. They call him Blackie. I am grateful to a kind Fate that had given the train-lifter the chance, between carrying locomotives, to see a Scotty in action. 🐾

Chips the War Dog

Chips, a German shepherd/collie/husky mix, was perhaps the most noted dog to take part in any war effort. At the height of WWII, he was assigned to the Third Military Police Platoon, Third Infantry Division in North Africa, Sicily, Italy, France, and Germany, where he served as a sentry dog, alerting the handler to the approach of enemies. In the predawn twilight of July 10, 1943, Chips and the Seventh Army, under the command of General Patton, boarded amphibious crafts off the coast of Licata, Sicily. Under heavy fire and trapped on the beach, Chips broke loose from his handlers, defying his training, and stormed a machine-gun nest, capturing an enemy soldier by the neck and sending several others scattering. Chips was taken to a hospital for scalp wounds, hip wounds, and powder burns in the mouth—perhaps evidence of direct contact with smoldering enemy firearms. He later received the Silver Star for bravery and the Purple Heart for wounds received in action, both from General Lucian Truscott. However, these awards were revoked when the military determined that Chips was classified as "equipment" and therefore ineligible to receive such honors. Upon returning home at the age of 6, he adapted smoothly to civilian life but passed away several months later from complications of his war injuries. 🐾

Baker Man, Baker Man, bake these crunchy, glazed-meat treats as fast as you can! Serve at your next obedience class, and be the envy of all the dog parents.

For treats:
1/2 pound ground beef or lamb
1/2 cup Italian-flavored bread crumbs
1 carrot, finely grated
1 egg, beaten
2 teaspoons grated Parmesan cheese
2 teaspoons tomato paste

For glaze:
1 egg
2 tablespoons chicken or beef broth or
    1 tablespoon milk

1. Preheat oven to 350°F.

2. Combine all ingredients for treats.

3. Form small, bite-size balls. Flatten slightly and place on a greased baking sheet.

4. Whisk egg and liquid together to make the glaze.

5. Bake 6–7 minutes. Remove from oven and brush on glaze. Bake 6–7 minutes more or until brown. Cool.

6. Refrigerate in an airtight container for up to 1 week, or freeze indefinitely.

Makes about 2–3 dozen treats

Patty-Cake Appetizers

Lassie

by Eric Knight

Had it been any other part of the day [it was nearly four o'clock], Lassie might have returned to Hynes as he bid her. It had been on one of the newly ordered walks, with Lassie going along obediently, that he wanted to show Lassie "who was boss." And so, quite needlessly, he suddenly tugged on the leash. The leash slipped over Lassie's head. She was free! It was time to go for the boy! She wheeled and began trotting away. There was nothing to tell her that the rendezvous she would keep was hundreds of miles away. She broke from her trot into a gentle lope.

Priscilla and her grandfather rode up the road and halted by the iron gate to the estate. "I'll open it," the girl said and swung it slowly back on its hinges. Hynes was shouting: "Close the gate, Miss Priscilla!" For a second she swung her weight back on it. But then she saw again a certain picture in her mind—of a village boy standing beside the meshed wire of a run, saying to his dog: "Bide here forever—and don't never come home no more." Priscilla began swinging the gate wide open. "Good-bye, Lassie," she said, softly. "Good-bye and—good luck!"

But now Lassie had learned one thing. She must keep away from men. That first night Lassie traveled steadily. Whenever a path ran to the south, she followed it. For the first four days Lassie traveled without pause, resting only during the nights. On the fifth day a new demand began to gnaw at her senses. It was the call of hunger. Suddenly, on the path she saw what her nose had warned her of—a weasel and by his side the freshly killed body of a rabbit. She came near, and picked up the game. She smelled it again. It smelled good. It was food.

So the dog went, day after day. She could not know that the instinctive straight line toward home would bring her to an impasse against the great lochs of Scotland. Yet at the shore of the great loch, Lassie did not surrender her purpose. Day after day she worked west. A week [later] the long loch stretched as a barrier that a dog could not understand.

She was moving more slowly now, for the pads of her feet were bruised and sore, and between those pads on the right forefoot a thorn was festering. The loch had narrowed to a river. Lassie looked at the white, tumbling water. Then, boldly springing, she launched her body far out into the water. Again and again the current tumbled her with crushing force. The current drew her down, and she disappeared. Then fighting, swimming, driving, she made the landing. At last she was free—free to go south.

Lassie

It was long past nightfall when she denned up where a clump of gorse arched over beside a field-wall. In the tumbling river she had broken one rib and bruised badly her hind leg. She could travel no farther. For six days she lay, almost without a move. From the festering sore the thorn had worked its way. Lassie cleaned the wound. Her bad hind leg hung, not touching the ground. Hobbling across the field, she found the streamlet and lapped—the first time she had drunk for a week. For two more days she rested there. But of food, she had none. Then, stiffly, she crossed the stream. Going slowly, she struck out to the south.

By the great Scottish industrial city the river is broad— and there are aged bridges that have carried traffic north and south for centuries. Over one of those busy bridges Lassie trotted. She went along the pavement to the south. She did not heed the truck pulling up beside her. Something was moving through the air. About her was a net that strangled her efforts. For a full minute she fought, slashing at the imprisoning web. But she was only held the tighter. A thong was being twisted about her muzzle. Another thong went about her neck, another was binding her legs together. She felt the net being

187

lifted; then she was being beaten over the head. And then the men halted their beating, for a voice came, very clear, from the crowd: "Here, you don't heave to treat that dog as savagely as that!"

"Very sorry, mum; but it's my duty. There's a lot of mad dogs around—and a dog catcher's got to do his duty."

The van drew into a courtyard [and] backed up tight against a raised entrance. Other dogs in the van had lifted their voices in clamor. But Lassie had lain still, like a captive queen among lesser prisoners. The man entered the van with a small leash. Down they came over the tailboard of the van, and he leaned down to unslip the leash. In that flash, Lassie was free. Down the corridor she went. Hands grabbed at her as she raced along. There were many doors, all closed. And then escape came. For one of the forbidding doors opened, and a voice sounded: "What's going on out here? Do you realize there's a Court of Law sitting . . ." That was as far as he got. For at that moment a tawny figure streaked by him. Then he shut the door. At last, in a corner, Lassie stood at bay. Bearing the net, the two men entered the court. "We'll soon ha' her out o' here, Your Lordship," one said. But as he spoke, Lassie wheeled away. Above her was an open window. She leaped to the ledge—and then stood there in hesitation. There was a sheer drop of twenty feet to concrete below. On the ledge Lassie trembled. Off to the left was the roof of the van only ten feet below. Then she leaped. Out she drove, as far as she could, toward the top of the van. Reaching out with her forelegs, she just touched. Then she dropped to the ground heavily; and she lay, stunned. The two men made their way to the courtyard. They looked about in amazement. She was not there. "Donnell, where is she?" "Gone for the wall, Mr. Fairgusson!" "Six foot—and she should be dead, Donnell."

Slowly, steadily, Lassie came across a field. She was going at a painful walk, still continuing to go south. The track became mud, then a puddle, and the puddle was the edge of a river. Lassie, wading forward tentatively, went deeper and deeper. She began swimming. And when at last she reached the other shore, she was almost too weak to climb the bank. There, at last, she dropped. But she was in England! Lassie lay on one side. Her eyes were glazed. Darkness came with its night sounds. Dawn came. Lassie rose slowly. She set out—going south.

Together they [Daniel and Dolly Fadden] hurried out into the night, leaning against the gusts of wind and rain. There she saw what her husband had found—a dog, lying in the ditch. "It's too done up to walk," he shouted. The two old people brought Lassie into the warmth of the hearth and laid her on the rug. "I doubt it'll live till the morn," the man said. Awkwardly the old man bent, rubbing the dog's drenched coat. Only dimly Lassie knew of the saucer of warm milk set beside her head. Then she felt her head being lifted. She gulped, once—twice—three times. Firmly the old woman planted herself in the rocking chair for a night a watching. A week later Mrs. Fadden looked over her glasses and beamed at Lassie, lying on the rug, her ears erect. Her beautiful dog, *her* dog! "Oh, if anyone owns it! Find out, will ye, Dan? Go ask around." It was a long afternoon. At last she heard footsteps. "I asked all around the place—everywhere—and nobody seems to ha' lost her." "Then she's ours!"

   Lassie lay on the rug. Strength had returned in the three weeks in her new home. The one driving force of her life was wakened. As the clock moved round toward four, it became maddening. Lassie went to the door. She whined and lifted her head. Then she began pacing back and forth. The woman shook her head. "I didn't tell ye, but the last three days, Dan, she's not eating. She's not happy. Dan, she's going somewhere. She's on her way." The next afternoon when the time neared four o'clock, and Lassie rose, their eyes followed her. And when Lassie whined at the door, they both sighed. The woman opened the door. Side by side, the old man and his wife followed Lassie out to the road. There for a moment the dog stood. For a second, the old woman wished to call the dog back. But she lifted her

head. "It's all right, then, dog. If ye must go—awa' wi' ye."
Lassie caught the word "go." She turned, looked back once
as in farewell, and then started across the field. She was
going south again. They went into the cottage and sat at the
table. But neither of them ate.

~

Lassie plodded on. Now she was crossing a great, high moor,
where the wind swept without halt. The snowstorm drove
from behind her. She found it hard to keep going. At last
she staggered and fell. The snow was too deep. She began
plunging at it like a horse, but before very long she found
herself utterly exhausted. She gave a long cry—the cry of a
dog lost, cold and helpless. Lassie sank to the ground. Below
that white blanket she lay, exhausted but warm.

It was a long way from Greenall Bridge to the Duke of
Rudling's place in Scotland. For an animal it would be a
thousand miles through strange terrain with nothing but
instinct to tell direction. Yet, in his heart Joe Carraclough
tried to believe that somehow his dog would be there some-
day, waiting by the school gate.

Always, when school ended, Joe tried to prepare himself
not to be disappointed, because there could be no dog there.
And so coming across the schoolyard that day, Joe could not
believe his eyes. There, walking the last few yards to the
gate was—his dog! He stood, for the coming of the dog was

terrible—a crawl rather than a walk. He raced across the
yard and fell to his knees. This was a dog that lay, weakly
trying to lift a head that would no longer lift. "I must get
her home quick!" the boy was saying. Ian Cawper stepped
forward. His great arms cradled the dog. Joe raced along the
street and burst into the cottage: "Mother! Father! Lassie's
come home!" Not a word did his parents speak to him.
Instead, they both worked over the dog. Joe watched how
his father spooned in the warm liquid, he saw how it
drooled out again. He saw his mother warm up a blanket
and wrap it round the dog. "Pneumonia," his father said at
last. "She's not strong enough now . . ." It was his mother
who seemed to be alive and strong. "I just *won't* be beat,"
she said. She took down a vase. The copper pennies came
into her hand. His father hurried out into the night. When
he came back he was carrying bundles—eggs and a small
bottle of brandy—precious and costly things in that home. In
the morning his mother was still on the rug, and the fire
was still burning warm. The dog, swathed in blankets, lay
quiet. That was one day. There was another when Joe's
mother sighed with pleasure, for as she prepared the milk,
the dog stirred. When the bowl was set down, she put down
her head and lapped. . . .

    The Duke of Rudling got out of a car. "Go away," the boy
said fiercely. "Thy tyke's not here. It's not Lassie." Then

they all heard the voice of Sam Carraclough: "Does it look like any dog that belongs to thee?" He saw his father standing with a dog the like of which few men had ever seen before. He understood. He knew that if a dog coper could treat a dog so its bad points came to look like good ones, he could also make its good ones look like bad ones. But the Duke knew many things too. Slowly he knelt down and picked up a forepaw. And those eyes stared steadily at the underside of the paw, seeing only the five black pads, crossed and recrossed with half-healed scars. "Sam Carraclough," he said. "This is no dog of mine. Not for a single second did she ever belong to me! Four hundred miles! I wouldn't ha' believed it." He turned. "You working? I need somebody at my kennels. And I think you must know—a lot—about dogs. So there. That's settled." It was afterward that the girl [Priscilla] said, "Grandfather, you are kind about the dog." "Nonsense," he growled. "For five years I've sworn I'd have that dog. And now I've got her." 🐾

Tales That Wag the Dog

BEAUTIFUL JOE, a real dog who inspired the bestselling 1893 Marshall Saunders novel by the same name • **BANGA**, from Mikhail Bulgakov's *The Master and Margarita* • **BIG RED**, **IRISH RED**, and other Irish setters from Jim Kjelgaard's novels • **BUCK**, from Jack London's *The Call of the Wild* • **BULLSEYE**, Bill Sikes's dog in Dickens's *Oliver Twist* • **FANG**, Hagrid's dog in J. K. Rowling's *Harry Potter* books • **THE HOUND OF THE BASKERVILLES**, from Arthur Conan Doyle's Sherlock Holmes story of the same name • **NANA**, a Newfoundland, from J. M. Barrie's *Peter Pan* • **ROWF** and **SNITTER**, from Richard Adams's *The Plague Dogs* • **WINN-DIXIE**, from Kate DiCamillo's *Because of Winn-Dixie* • **TIMMY**, from Enid Blyton's *Famous Five* series • **LAD**, the collie from the legendary stories of Albert Payson Terhune • **YELLOW DOG DINGO**, from Rudyard Kipling's *Just So Stories* • **PATRASCHE**, from Ouida's *A Dog of Flanders* • **WHAT-A-MESS**, the Afghan puppy from Frank Muir's children's books • **WHITE FANG**, from Jack London's novel of the same name • **WELLINGTON**, from Mark Haddon's *The Curious Incident of the Dog in the Night-Time* • **SIRIUS**, from Olaf Stapledon's sci-fi novel of the same name • **MONTMORENCY**, from Jerome K. Jerome's *Three Men in a Boat (To Say Nothing of the Dog!)* • **BONNIE BLUE** and **PROMISE**, from James H. Street's *The Biscuit Eater* • **NOP**, a border collie, from Donald McCaig's novel *Nop's Trials* • **JACK**, from Laura Ingalls Wilder's *Little House on the Prairie* • **HUAN**, the great wolfhound of Valinor, from J. R. R. Tolkien's novel *The Silmarillion* • **HOWARD**, from James Howe's *Bunnicula* • **GASPODE**, from Terry Pratchett's *Discworld* novels •

TOTO, from L. Frank Baum's *The Wonderful Wizard of Oz*

Dog Sayings . . .
And What They Mean

He who lies down with dogs rises with fleas.

Some people have bad habits, just like dogs have fleas. If you spend too much time with them, you'll get them, too.

Let sleeping dogs lie.

It's best to just leave old disagreements alone.

You're in the doghouse!

When you're in some sort of trouble because of some wrong you did or are suspected of doing.

You're barking up the wrong tree.

You're looking in the wrong place.

You can't teach an old dog new tricks.

When people are used to doing things a certain way, they don't like to change.

Ode To The Dog

by Pablo Neruda

The dog is asking me a question
and I have no answer.
He dashed through the countryside and asks me
wordlessly,
and his eyes
are two moist question marks, two wet
inquiring flames,
but I do not answer
because I haven't got the answer.
I have nothing to say.
Dog and man: together we roam
the open countryside.

Leaves shine as
if someone
had kissed them
one by one,
orange trees

rise up from the earth
raising
minute planetariums
in trees that are as rounded
and green as the night,
while we roam together, dog and man
sniffing everything, jostling clover
in the countryside of Chile,
cradled by the bright fingers of September.
The dog makes stops,
chases bees,
leaps over restless water,
listens to far-off
barking,
pees on a rock,
and presents me the tip of his snout
as if it were a gift:
it is the freshness of his love,
his message of love.
And he asks me
with both eyes:
why is it daytime? why does night always fall?

why does spring bring
nothing
in its basket
for wandering dogs
but useless flowers,
flowers and more flowers?
This is how the dog
asks questions
and I do not reply.

Together we roam,
man and dog bound together again
by the bright green morning,
by the provocative empty solitude
in which we alone
exist,
this union of dog and dew
or poet and woods.
For these two companions,
for these fellow-hunters,
there is no lurking fowl
or secret berry

but only birdsong and sweet smells,
a world moistened
by night's distillations,
a green tunnel and then
    a meadow,
        a gust of orangey air,
            the murmurings of roots,
            life on the move,
                breathing and growing,
                and the ancient friendship,
                the joy
                    of being dog or being man
                    fused
                    in a single beast
                    that pads along on
                    six feet,
                    wagging
                    its dew-wet tail.

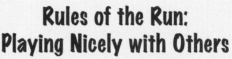

Rules of the Run:
Playing Nicely with Others

*Your dog is the scourge of the doggy playground. No matter what you do,
he refuses to get along with the other dogs, and scares the other owners.
He chases everything and everyone that moves, including vehicles, children, joggers, and the family cat. Before you tuck your figurative tail
between your legs in embarrassment, try these suggestions.*

Fighting

DO ascertain that your dog has achieved reliable bite moderation
(see Soften the Bite, page 113). If your full-grown or adoles-
cent dog does not have bite control, consult a trainer. If he plays with
your kids, if he bites but never hard enough to break the skin, chances
are that he will not injure another dog even if he gets into a fight.
Fights tend to be a lot of noise and little else.

Have friends bring their dogs for controlled visits. Make sure
guests understand that your dog is not dangerous. The sniffing of private parts is "play nice" behavior and should be rewarded immediately
with a treat. Likewise, you can stop the baring of teeth by making a
loud noise such as a clap and giving the growler a treat once he is distracted. Food can take the wind out of an impending doggy squall.

DON'T neglect to train, train, train the aggressive pooch. The
more activities she learns, the happier and more con-
fident she will be, and the less interest she will have in victimizing
other animals.

Chasing

DO teach your dog Take It and Leave It (p. 320). These can be generalized to mean "Get the ball," "Leave Tommy's guinea pig alone," or "Drop that jogger!"

If your dog not only chases things but actually nips or grabs hold, then you have an animal with a strong prey drive indeed. Consult a trainer who specializes in deprogramming. The trainer might have you try squirting a citronella-spray deterrent at the dog out the window of your slow-moving car.

DON'T carry chicken in your pocket to toss at the dog when she chases you, the way some joggers advise. You will only be rewarding her bad behavior! Instead, invest in citronella spray. It smells terrible to the dog and is harmless.

A Letter to the ASPCA

by E. B. White

E. B. White penned the following letter to the ASPCA in response to receiving a notice that his dog, Minnie, was illegally unlicensed.

12 April 1951
The American Society for the Prevention of Cruelty to Animals
York Avenue and East 92nd Street
New York, 28, NY

Dear Sirs:

I have your letter, undated, saying that I am harboring an unlicensed dog in violation of the law. If by "harboring" you mean getting up two or three times every night to pull Minnie's blanket up over her, I am harboring a dog all right. The blanket keeps slipping off. I suppose you are wondering by now why I don't get her a sweater instead. That's a joke on you. She has a knitted sweater, but she doesn't like to wear it for sleeping; her legs are so short they work out of a sweater and her toenails get caught in the mesh, and this disturbs her rest. If Minnie doesn't get her rest, she feels it right away. I do myself, and of course with this night duty of mine, the way the blanket slips and all, I haven't had any real rest in years. Minnie is twelve.

In spite of what your inspector reported, she has a license. She is licensed in the state of Maine as an unspayed bitch, or what is more commonly called an "unspaded" bitch. She wears her metal license tag but I must say I don't particularly care for it, as it is in the shape of a hydrant, which seems to me a feeble gag, besides being pointless in the case of a female. It is hard to believe that any state in the Union would circulate a gag like that and make people pay money for it, but Maine is always thinking of something. Maine puts up roadside crosses along the highways to mark the spots where people have lost their lives in motor accidents, so the highways are beginning to take on the appearance of a cemetery, and motoring in Maine has become a solemn experience, when one thinks mostly about death. I was driving along a road near Kittery the other day thinking about death and all of a sudden I heard the spring peepers. That changed me right away and I suddenly thought about life. It was the nicest feeling.

You asked about Minnie's name, sex, breed, and phone number. She doesn't answer the phone. She is a dachshund and can't reach it, but she wouldn't answer it even if she could, as she has no interest in outside calls. I did have a dachshund once, a male, who was interested in the telephone, and who got a great many calls, but Fred was an exceptional dog (his name was Fred) and I can't think of anything offhand that he wasn't interested in. The telephone was only one of a thousand things. He loved life—that is, he loved life if by "life" you mean "trouble," and of course the phone is almost synonymous with trouble. Minnie loves life, too, but her idea of life is a warm bed, preferably with an electric pad, and a friend in bed with her, and plenty of shut-eye, night and days. She's almost twelve. I guess I've already mentioned that. I got her from Dr. Clarence Little in 1939. He was using dachshunds in his cancer-research experiments (that was before Winchell was running the thing) and he had a couple of extra puppies, so I wheedled Minnie out of him. She later had puppies by her own father, at Dr. Little's request. What do you think about that for scandal? I know what Fred thought about it. He was some put out.

Sincerely yours,
E. B. White

Kibbles 'n Bits
Dog Heroes of the Year

Since 1954, Kibbles 'n Bits has been honoring ordinary dogs for their out-standing achievements. The Dog Hero of the Year award focuses on brav-ery, intelligence, and loyalty, celebrating when man's best friend ventures far beyond simple companionship to sheer heroism. The following fearless canines have saved drowning victims, alerted families to fires, protected owners from wild animals, found missing persons, and performed many other incredible acts.

1980 **"Woodie," Cleveland, Ohio** A mixed breed named Woodie broke a hip when he leaped from an 80-foot cliff to rescue his owner's fiancé, Ray, from drowning. Ray fell from the cliff and landed facedown in a shallow river. Woodie nudged his face above water until help arrived.

1981 **"King," Granite Falls, Washington** When a house fire broke out, the Carlson's mixed breed clawed and chewed through a plywood door in order to alert the entire family.

1982 **"Bo," Glenwood Springs, Colorado** Bo and his owner, Laurie, were riding the rapids on the Colorado River when their raft overturned. Bo, a Labrador retriever, pulled Laurie by the hair out from under the raft and swam to shore with Laurie holding on to his tail.

1983 **"Villa," Villas, New Jersey** During a severe blizzard, 60-mile-per-hour winds blew 11-year-old Andrea into a large snowdrift about 40 feet from her home. Villa, a Newfoundland, heard Andrea's calls for help and leaped a 5-foot fence to rescue her snowbound neighbor.

1984 **"Leo," Hunt, Texas** This poodle received six poisonous snakebites while protecting two children from a diamondback snake.

1985 **"Tango," Port Townsend, Washington** Tango, a 12-year-old mixed breed, rescued his owner, Al, when a frightened cow attacked him. Tango intervened, and Al crawled away.

1986 **"Champ" and "Buddy," Dickinson, North Carolina** Together, this terrier and mixed breed led their owners to a nearby warehouse where an injured truck driver was trapped beneath a 2,680-pound earth mover tire.

1987 **"Jet," Sepulveda, California** This Doberman pinscher obtained medical help for her owner who suffered from severe hypoglycemia.

1988 **"Buppy," Burlington, New Jersey** This mixed breed burned his nose and singed his coat while ensuring that his owner's disabled grandmother escaped from her burning house.

1989 **"Reona," Watsonville, California** During the San Francisco earthquake, a rottweiler saved a frightened 5-year-old neighbor with epilepsy. Reona pushed the child aside just before a microwave oven fell from the top of a refrigerator. The dog then calmed the young girl, possibly sparing her from a seizure.

1990 **"Chelsea," Houston, Texas** Putting her own life on the line, this golden retriever rescued her owner and a neighbor from two gunmen. Chelsea lunged at the gunmen and was shot in the shoulder. She recovered fully.

213

Kibbles 'n Bits Dog Heroes of the Year

1991 **"Sheena," St. Petersburg, Florida and "Willy," Mehlville, Missouri** (two winners) When Sheena's disabled owner was attacked by two men in a parking lot, this once-abandoned mixed breed lunged at the assailants, knocking one to the ground and chasing the other away. Willy, a 9-year-old Weimaraner saved his owner's life when a faulty furnace in her home leaked carbon monoxide. Willy pawed at his owner to awaken her from a deep sleep and barked frantically until she escaped from the house.

1992 **"Sparky," Tullahoma, Tennessee** When Sparky's burly 227-pound owner, Bo, collapsed from a heart attack on a morning walk, this 130-pound yellow Labrador retriever dragged his master home nearly 200 yards. Thanks to Sparky's quick actions, Bo made it to the hospital just in time for his condition to be stabilized.

1993 **"Weela," Imperial Beach, California** During large-scale flooding in Southern California's Tijuana River valley, Weela's repeated heroism over a 3-month period saved 30 people, 29 dogs, 13 horses and 1 cat, all of whom otherwise may have perished in the flood.

1994 **"Girl," Martins Ferry, Ohio** This loyal German shepherd sought help for her owner who was bleeding to death when knocked unconscious while cutting trees with a chainsaw.

1995 **"Bailey," Springfield, Missouri** Bailey attacked a 2,000-pound bull that had charged and pinned his owner. Bailey's attack gave his injured owner enough time to crawl under a fence to safety.

1996 **"Brandy," Tucson, Arizona** After being shot five times by a home invader, Brandy kept fighting and chased the attacker out, saving her owner's life.

Kibbles 'n Bits Dog Heroes of the Year

1999 **"Sadie," Beth Page, Tennessee** Sadie and her owner, Michael, went on a routine trip in the woods near their home. En route, Sadie's owner collapsed from a severe heart attack. Sadie, weighing only 45 pounds, dragged her unconscious 180-pound owner all the way home and barked until his wife came to the door. Michael was rushed to a hospital, where a life-saving triple-bypass surgery was performed.

2000 **"Shelby," Ely, Iowa** On the evening of December 13, after a long day of baking cookies, John and Janet Walderbach and their friends' two children were nearly overcome by carbon monoxide which had filled the house. Shelby, their 7-year-old German shepherd, revived the couple and showed signs of distress until John, Janet, and the children realized the danger and went outside the home to safety.

2001 **"Biyou," Dale, Ohio** Biyou, a 3-year-old half Australian shepherd/half wolf from Richmond Dale, Ohio, saved her owner from drowning in an icy creek and freezing from exposure.

2002 **"Blue," La Belle, Florida** Two-year-old Blue, an Australian blue heeler, saved his 85-year-old owner from an alligator attack and survived numerous injuries from the dangerous encounter.

2003 **"Bullet," Bellport, New York** Sixteen-year-old Bullet, a golden retriever whose family opted for cancer surgery for her instead of euthanasia, survived and went on to save the family's 20-day-old son when she alerted his mom to the baby's asphyxiation in the nick of time.

2004 **"Sundance," Farmingville, New York** Sundance, a golden retriever, saved two young daughters from an 8-foot ball python in their toy-ball play pit.

215

Preserving the Novelty

Tips for Keeping It Fresh

1. Rotate your dog's toy collection once in a while. Put away old bones and squeaky toys and bring out a new set. They may not seem very dissimilar to you, but they will smell different and exciting to your dog.

2. Respond to your dog when she shows up to get your attention with a toy or if she spontaneously does a trick for you. These are the treats dogs give to humans. They enjoy when we are pleased.

3. Put away one of her favorite toys in a spot where she can find it. See how many hours or days elapse before your dog shows up with it in her mouth and invites you to play.

4. Generalize your dog's behavior to other people. Let a friend throw a Frisbee, take him for a walk, or work with you on obedience. Have your dog show his new friend how he sits, and let your friend reward him. Get your pup used to strangers. Train a neighborhood teen in doggie etiquette. If Fido is well behaved, introduce him to other dogs or take him to visit a friend's house.

5. Take your dog to a new location to play catch.

6. Generalize your dog's behavior to other locations. Take her where there are distractions, such as your front sidewalk or public park, and practice obedience training. Be sure to reward your dog when she does something you like!

7. Take your pooch on an errand with you. Folks have been known to take dogs for rides in bike baskets. Just be sure that your pooch is extra secure and that you stay away from dangerous roads and heavy traffic.

8. Vary your walks to different neighborhoods and at different speeds.

The Dog Book
by Albert Payson Terhune

THE COCKER SPANIEL

Queen was a cocker spaniel of no specially lofty pedigree. She belonged to a grocer in Columbus, Ohio. Her owner had the sense to understand her nature and to give her an education, which she was quick to absorb. One of the first things he taught her was to mail his letters. Many dogs will retrieve their owners' mail from the carriers, but few have been taught to post it. Queen did it perfectly, and always took the keenest pride and delight in acting as mail-carrier.

The mail was put in a basket. Around Queen's neck was slung a little placard which read: PLEASE MAIL MY LETTERS IN THIS BOX. The cocker took the basket in her mouth and trotted away to the nearest mail-box. This was on a lamp-post at a busy corner, nearly a half-mile away from the grocery. There, with the basket still in her mouth and the placard around her neck, she would sit up on her hind legs, and wag her tail invitingly at every passer-by who stopped to look at her.

Within a minute or two, someone would be certain to take the bundle of mail out of the basket and drop it into the box. Then, wagging her tail still more briskly in gratitude, Queen would run home with the empty basket. In all the hundreds of times she performed this trick, never was a letter lost.

Her master also taught her to know the names and the addresses of the few tradesmen with whom he dealt. He would give her a basket and tell her to go to his butcher. Not once would she go to the wrong place. Into the butcher shop she would run with her basket. The butcher would read the order list lying in the bottom of it, and place the provisions in the basket for Queen to carry safely back home. The same thing happened at other stores.

No matter how hungry she might be, and no matter how tempting the food in the basket might smell, she would not tough a mouthful of it; and she fought fiercely to defend it whenever some other dog or some man tried to rob her of it.

THE SETTER

Once when I was a boy, my father an I were quail-shooting with my father's staunch old setter, Frank. The dog was in front of us quartering the stubble field, working away happily, with tail waving and nose almost touching the ground. A railroad track ran through the middle of the big field. As Frank came within about eighteen inches of the track, he halted and stiffened all over, with one forefoot tucked up. He was pointing something in a thick tuft of grass just across the track, and waiting for my father to order him to go ahead. A good hunting dog does not break his point without orders, and old Frank was the very best.

Just then an express train came tearing around a curve at top

speed. For a moment I thought the locomotive was going to hit the dog. He must have thought so, too, for it came thundering toward him in a swirl of dust and smoke and cinders. Such a sight was enough to scare any dog and make him back away. But Frank did not stir. When the train had whizzed past, missing his rigid nose by perhaps only an inch or so, filling his sensitive nostrils with cinders and black smoke, and stinging him with its shower of hot sparks, there he stood motionless as a statue, his forefoot tucked up, body and tail rigid. He still pointed the unseen occupant of the patch of grass, and waited for my father's command.

At a word from my father, Frank took a hesitant step forward, then another. Out from the tuft of long grass a quail flew up. I don't know why it had not flown up when the train passed; perhaps it was too badly frightened. As it rocketed from the hiding place whence his slow advance had driven it, Frank dropped to the ground, as he had been taught to do when a bird broke cover.

My father shot the fast-flying quail; then gave Frank another order. Instantly the setter dashed forward and retrieved the fallen bird, carrying it as tenderly in his mouth as if it had been a cushion full of pins. He trotted back to my father and dropped the quail gently into the wide-open pocket of his hunting coat. He seemed to take great pride in this simple trick.

That is all there is to the story. I have told it because it shows several things. First, the perfect training and the courage that kept Frank at his post of duty even when death seemed to be thundering down upon him; then the skill at retrieving; and, most of all, the unerring power of scent which made him locate the unseen bird and which enabled him to keep at the point when cinders and smoke were almost suffocating him.

THE SCOTTISH TERRIER

His name was Roddy. He belonged to my sister, whose summer home adjoins Sunnybank. Roddy was small, even for a Scottie. But his tiny body held the heart of a lion. Sometimes one or two of my biggest collies would follow me when I went to see my sister. As soon as these giants crossed the boundary line into her land, Roddy was on the job as an official watchdog.

He would rush out of the house, bristling with rage, and dash at the collies. Straight up to them he would charge, intent on driving them from the premises. He was a wise little dog, and he must have realized that any one of the collies could have killed him with a single bite, but it was his duty to defend his owner's land from marauders.

If the Sunnybank collies had been dogs of certain other breeds, it might have gone hard with valiant Roddy. But my experience has been that not one collie in five hundred will harm a dog so much smaller than himself.

As Roddy leaped up in a vain effort to reach their throats, the Sunnybank dogs would stand looking amusedly down at him,

waving their plumed tails. From one to another of them he would rush, challenging each to mortal combat. Then, when they would neither fight nor run away, he would glare at them in utter disgust, and trot angrily back to the house. It was no use. He had done his best to be a murderously dangerous watchdog.

He felt as you or I might have, if we had dared the Statue of Liberty to step down from her pedestal and fight us, and she had merely smiled and stayed where she was.

But Roddy's courage was as flamingly bright as if they actually had attacked him. He was on guard of his owner's home. And he was as fearless a guard as if he had fifty times his size and strength.

THE GREAT DANE

In my youth, a druggist on Sixth Avenue in New York City owned a glorious dark gray Great Dane named Jake. The dog used to be standing in front of the drug store when I passed there on my way to and from the office. I used to stop and talk to him and to his master; and we three got to be good friends.

Jake was as gentle as he was fearless. He was loved by everyone in the neighborhood. When charity drives were in progress, his master used to tie a little basket with a placard on it, to Jake's neck; and the dog would pace solemnly up and down the street. That was before the days of motor-cars, so Jake's rambles were safe from disaster. He would return home with the basket full of coins and bills, for few pedestrians could resist his friendly state-

225

liness when he approached them for alms. I don't know how many hundred dollars he collected for charity from time to time, but the amount was so great that all the local newspapers made mention of it.

Jake slept in a little room behind the store, the same room in which the druggist kept his safe. As the man was interested in many charities, the safe often contained a goodly sum of money. This fact became known, and two robbers decided to take advantage of it.

One night, they broke into the store and made their way to the back room where the safe was. But the safe's staunch guard was there, too. Jake met them on the threshold. Gone was his usual friendliness. He was guarding his owner's property. Roaring in anger, he charged the two intruders. They were panic-stricken. There was no time for them to escape, so they drew their pistols and opened fire on the attacking dog. Their bullets riddled his body. But he inflicted terrible punishment on them, before the sound of the shots and of his growling brought the nearest policeman on the run to the drug store.

The thieves were captured, thanks to the Great Dane's strength and courage and loyalty. But Jake had saved his master's treasure at the cost of his own life. He died from the bullet wounds he received during the battle. All the neighborhood mourned him. 🐾

Canine Crackups

When Good Dogs Go and Crossbreed

Pointer + setter =
Poinsetter, a traditional Christmas pet

Great Pyrenees + dachshund =
Pyradachs, a puzzling breed

Pekingese + Lhasa apso =
Peekasso, an abstract dog

Terrier + Bulldog =
Terribull, a dog prone to awful mistakes

Malamute + pointer =
Moot point, owned by . . . oh, well, it doesn't matter anyway

Newfoundland + basset hound =
Newfound asset hound, a dog for financial advisors

Bull terrier + shih tzu =
Bullshitz, a gregarious but unreliable breed

Canine Crackups

The Well-Bred Dog

Today, there are more than 700 types of purebred dogs, many originally bred for specific work activities. Here are but a few specialized breeds.

SAINT BERNARDS were trained to rescue lost travelers in the Alps.

BORDER COLLIES were bred to herd livestock—but will settle for herding anything that moves, including children and other pets.

BULLDOGS were bred to bait and fight bulls and bears, hence the short (hard-to-grab-on-to) snout.

NEWFOUNDLANDS, with their webbed feet for swimming, were bred to accompany ships' crew.

DACHSHUNDS were bred to kill badgers in their dens, while small terriers were bred as ratters.

POODLES were the foremost sight hounds and swimmers, and in fact the pom-pom haircut that we find so "swishy" actually was an effort to increase swimming speed while insulating the dog's joints from the cold.

Louis Doberman, a German tax collector, developed the **DOBERMAN** in the 1860s to act as his bodyguard while he worked.

Used for heavy draft work, the **ALASKAN MALAMUTE** is a heavy-boned dog with a steady, tireless gait.

The **SPRINGER SPANIEL** is prized not for springing on its prey, but for its ability to cause game birds to "spring up" out of the brush.

Teaching the INSTANT RECALL

The ability to call your dog instantly to you is especially important when around dangerous streets, when a dogfight is brewing, or when you simply need her to come inside. If your canine escape artist is running amok in the neighborhood, it may be next to impossible to distract him from his misbehavior—unless he knows the instant recall.

There are several ways to teach this, including playing the Recall Game, using a dog clicker, or luring with food. Whatever tools you use, it's important to put this behavior on a variable reinforcement schedule once your dog has it down, so that he will come even when you have no treats. If you begin to give the treat reinforcement at random so that your dog does not get food after each repetition the behavior will become that much stronger. He will be expecting the treat eventually; he just won't know when!

1. Begin by luring with food or rapping on the floor or wall; say "Come!" and treat when your pup comes to check it out. If you do not use a clicker you must treat immediately. If you use a clicker, click the moment she arrives and before you give the treat. (The clicker signals the dog immediately, yet allows you to keep the treats across the room and not on your person.)
2. Since it's difficult to do repetitions of the recall while you are holding food (your pooch will simply follow you when you try to walk away), it helps to either use another person or have the dog know a reliable sit. Take turns with the other person. Say your pup's name

and "Come!" Treat, and have the dog sit while you move away, or have your friend call him.

3. Repeat until he gets it. Have a short training session of 20 repetitions each day.

4. Be sure to practice the recall religiously and in various strange environments. Gradually increase the distraction level so that your dog comes to you under any circumstances. This process is called generalization. One famous animal-training couple was fond of taking their obedience-trained dogs—and cats—to an airport terminal for a workout. Imagine the sight of Puff or Spot on a tear down the length of Concourse B—not to catch a flight, but to get to his trainer!

Dogs And Weather

by Winifred Welles

I'd like a different dog
   For every kind of weather—
A narrow greyhound for a fog,
   A wolfhound strange and white,
With a tail like a silver feather
   To run with in the night,
When snow is still, and winter stars are bright.

In the fall I'd like to see
   In answer to my whistle,
A golden spaniel look at me.
   But best of all for rain
A terrier, hairy as a thistle,
   To trot with fine disdain
Beside me down the soaked, sweet-smelling lane.

TO DAY
FAIR, DRY
& WARM

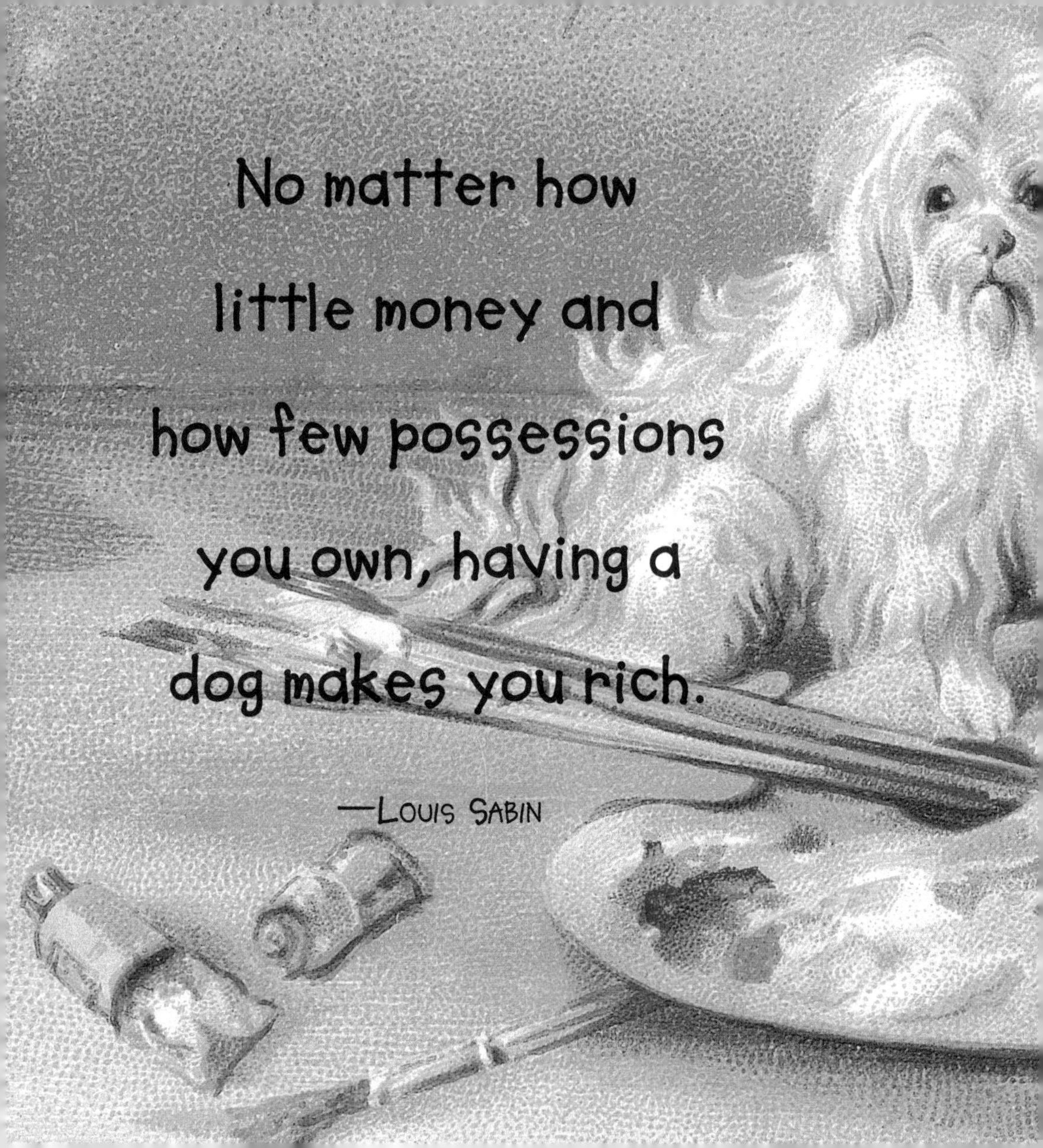

No matter how

little money and

how few possessions

you own, having a

dog makes you rich.

—LOUIS SABIN

Blood Will Tell

by Don Marquis

I am a middle-size dog, with spots on me here and there, and several different colors of hair mixed in even where there aren't any spots, and my ears are frazzled a little on the ends where they have been chewed in fights.

At first glance you might not pick me for an aristocrat. But I am one. I was considerably surprised when I discovered it, as nothing in my inmost feelings up to that time, nor in the treatment which I had received from dogs, humans, or boys, had led me to suspect it.

I can well remember the afternoon on which the discovery was made. A lot of us dogs were lying in the grass, up by the swimming hole, just lazying around, and the boys were doing the same. All the boys were naked and comfortable, and no humans were about, the only thing near being a cow or two and some horses, and although large they are scarcely more human than boys. Everybody had got tired of swimming, and it was too hot to drown out gophers or fight bumblebees, and the boys were smoking grapevine cigarettes and talking.

Us dogs was listening to the boys talk. A Stray Boy, by which I mean one not claimed or looked out for or owned by any dog, says to Freckles Watson, who is my boy:

"What breed would you call that dog of yours, Freck?"

I pricked up my ears at that. I cannot say that I had ever
set great store by breeds up to the time that I found out I was
an aristocrat myself, believing, as Bill Patterson, a human
and the town drunkard, used to say when intoxicated, that
often an honest heart beats beneath the outcast's ragged coat.

"Spot ain't any *one* particular breed," says Freckles. "He's
considerably mixed."

"He's a mongrel," says Squint Thompson, who is Jack
Thompson's boy.

"He ain't," says Freckles, so huffy that I saw a mongrel
must be some sort of a disgrace. "You're a link, link liar, and
so's your Aunt Mariar, and you're another."

"A dog," chips in the Stray Boy, "has either got to be a
thoroughbred or a mongrel. He's either an aristocrat or else
he's a common dog."

"Spot ain't any common dog," says Freckles, sticking up
for me. "He can lick any dog in town within five pounds of
his weight."

"He's got some spaniel in him," says the Stray Boy.

"His nose is pointed like a hound's nose," says Squint
Thompson.

"Well," says Freckles, "neither one of them kind of dogs is
a common dog."

"Spot has got some bulldog blood in him, too," says Tom
Mulligan, an Irish boy owned by a dog by the name of Mutt
Mulligan. "Did you ever notice how Spot will hang on so

you can't pry him loose, when he gets into a fight?"

"That proves he is an aristocratic kind of dog," says Freckles.

"There's some bird-dog blood in Spot," says the Stray Boy, sizing me up careful.

"He's got some collie in him, too," says Squint Thompson. "His voice sounds just like a collie's when he barks."

"But his tail is more like a coach dog's tail," says Tom Mulligan.

"His hair ain't, though," says the Stray Boy. "Some of his hair is like a setter's."

"His teeth are like a mastiff's," says Mutt Mulligan's boy Tom. And they went on like that; I never knew before there were so many different kinds of thoroughbred dog. Finally Freckles says:

"Yes, he's got all them different kinds of thoroughbred blood in him, and he's got other kinds you ain't mentioned and that you ain't slick enough to see. You may think you're running him down, but what you say just *proves* he ain't a common dog." I was glad to hear that. It was beginning to look to me that they had a pretty good case for me being a mongrel.

"How does it prove it?" asked the Stray Boy.

"Well," says Freckles, "you know who the king of Germany is, don't you?"

They said they'd heard of him from time to time.

"Well," says Freckles, "if you were a relation of the king of Germany you'd be a member of the German royal family.

241

You fellows may not know that, but you would. You'd be a swell, a regular high-mucky-muck."

They said they guessed they would.

"Now, then," says Freckles, "if you were a relation to the king of Switzerland, too, you'd be just *twice* as swell, wouldn't you, as if you were only related to *one* royal family? Plenty of people are related to just *one* royal family."

Tom Mulligan butts in and says that way back, in the early days, his folks was the kings of Ireland; but no one pays any attention.

"Suppose, then, you're a cousin of the queen of England into the bargain and your granddad was king of Scotland, and the prince of Wales and the emperor of France and the sultan of Russia and the rest of those royalties were relations of yours, wouldn't all that royal blood make you *twenty times* as much of a high-mucky-muck as if you had just *one* measly little old king for a relation?"

The boys had to admit that it would.

"You wouldn't call a fellow with all that royal blood in him a *mongrel*, would you?" says Freckles. "You bet your sweet life you wouldn't! A fellow like that is darned near on the level with a congressman or a vice-president. Whenever he travels around in the old country they turn out the brass band; and the firemen and the Knights of Pythias and the Modern Woodmen parade, and the mayor makes a speech, and there's a picnic and firecrackers, and he gets blamed

near anything he wants. People kowtow to him, just like they do to a swell left-handed pitcher or a champion prize fighter. If you went over to the old country and called a fellow like that a mongrel, and it got out on you, you would be sent to jail for it."

Tom Mulligan says yes, that is so; his granddad came to this country through getting into some kind of trouble about the king of England, and the king of England ain't anywhere near as swell as the fellow Freckles described, nor near so royal, neither.

"Well, then," says Freckles, "it's the same way with my dog Spot here. *Any* dog can be full of just *one* kind of thoroughbred blood. That's nothing! But Spot here has got more different kinds of thoroughbred blood in him than any dog you ever saw. By your own say-so he has. He's got *all* kinds of thoroughbred blood in him. If there's any kind he ain't got, you just name it, will you?"

"He ain't got any Great Dane in him," yells the Stray Boy, hating to knuckle under.

"You're a liar—he has, too," says Freckles.

The Stray Boy backed it, and there was a fight. All us dogs and boys gathered around in a ring to watch it, and I was more anxious than anybody else. For the way that fight went, it was easy to see, would decide what I was.

Well, Freckles licked that Stray Boy, and rubbed his nose in the mud, and that's how I come to be an aristocrat. 🐾

The Dollar Dog
by John Ciardi

A dollar dog is all mixed up.
A bit of this, a bit of that.
We got ours when he was a pup
So small he slept in an old hat.
So small we borrowed a doll's beads
To make him his first collar.
Too small to see how many breeds
We got for just one dollar.
But not at all too small to see
He had an appetite.
An appetite? It seems to me
He ate up everything in sight!

Tang the Guardian

Before his adoption by a good family in Denison, Texas, Tang, an enormous and loveable collie, had been severely abused and, as a result, completely distrusted humans—especially children. However, his new family sensed that Tang had a big heart deep within and set out to transform the cautious collie into a fluffy bundle of courage. With the family's persistent love and nurturing, Tang not only overcame his misgivings, he transformed into an incredibly perceptive hero. On four separate occasions, Tang leapt in front of oncoming traffic, stopping vehicles to guide young children out of the roadway and into safety. During a fifth incident in 1954, Tang staged a protest in front of a milk truck, barking objections until the bewildered driver succumbed and checked his cargo. There stood a 2-year-old girl who had climbed into the hold and had been in great danger of falling out. Upon her removal, Tang ceased his protest and lay calmly on the sidewalk. 🐾

These dog cookies are not only delectable but healthy, too, including the iron and nutrients of liver, one of dogs' favorite foods. For softer treats—especially for older dogs—reduce the cooking time to 30 minutes and leave out the glaze.

For cookies:
1 pound raw beef or chicken liver, beaten to a pulp with a fork
1 egg
1 cup wheat flour
$^1/_2$ cup bread crumbs
$^1/_4$ teaspoon oregano

For glaze:
1 egg
2 tablespoons chicken or beef broth or 1 tablespoon milk

1. Preheat oven to 350°F.

2. Mix cookie ingredients well. Form into small balls, place on a greased baking sheet, and bake for about 20 minutes.

3. Whisk egg and liquid together to make the glaze.

4. Remove cookies from oven and brush on glaze. Turn and glaze the other side. Return to oven for another 20 minutes, or until crisp.

5. Cool on racks. Refrigerate in an airtight container for up to 1 week, or freeze indefinitely.

Makes several dozen small treats

Homemade Liver Snaps

A Woman's Best Friend

by Erica Jong

"We have been here so short a time/and we pretended we have invented memory," W.S. Merwin writes in his poem "Elders," speaking of human hubris among the animals. We humans like to flatter ourselves that we are smarter than the animals with whom we share our lives. But really we love them for their wisdom, which is born of innocence. Dogs have no guile. Even vicious dogs as Dobermans and Pit Bulls have no guile. They don't profess to love your work and then attack it. They don't lick you, then bite to draw blood. In a world of hypocrisy and betrayal, dogs are direct. They never lie.

They think with their noses, and the nose is the most primitive and infallible organ. If we could live by our sense of smell, our lives would be much simpler. Other organs— eyes, genitals—betray, but the nose never lies. Dogs have infallible bullshit detectors. *They can even, we think, smell our cancer.* Moreover, they heed *their noses* as humans never do. We love dogs because they show us how to live with utmost simplicity: Rejoice and kick up your heels after a good shit. Love the one who feeds you. Curl up with the one that strokes your belly. Cherish a good master and lick him into enduring servitude. Celebrate life. Praise God. Find your way home no matter how long it takes. Watch out for the coyotes in the woods. Sniff every corner of the room before you decide to stay there. Turn around three times and create a magic circle before you settle down to dreaming. Decide to trust someone totally before you die.

These are some of things I have learned from the dogs in my life. Cats teach others lessons—lessons about keeping your own counsel, cherishing your independence, and giving love without surrendering one's self. Dogs seem more slobbery and slavish. But it is we who become their slaves. As a species, humans are slow to trust. Perhaps it is because we have disregarded our noses for so many millennia. The nose is the only organ that tells it true. By living with dogs, we reclaim the feral in ourselves. We may seek to civilize them, but in truth they help us to reclaim the wildness in ourselves. They remind us that in ancient days we had much wisdom that we have since sadly abandoned: the wisdom of touch, the wisdom of smell, the wisdom of the senses.

These days I divide my weeks between Connecticut and Manhattan. When I want to work with the peace that comes only from long days alone, without the dynamo of the city whirring in my ears, I go to Connecticut, pray for snow, and retreat to my studio on stilts to work on my novel. *I cannot do this without* my dog.

Belinda Barkawitz, my big black standard poodle, is becoming an exemplary muse. I feel safe in the country without a human companion as long as she is there to be my early warning system. I rely on the fact that her nose and ears are sharper than mine are. I know she will bark long before the doorbell rings and keep me apprised of who is coming down my driveway—whether deer or delivery truck.

She has an I-thou relationship with every tree on my property so she constantly reminds me of how precious and singular each one is. The birches bend for her. The hemlocks drop their weighty armfuls of snow on *her head*. Circling each one, she kicks up her heels like a creature that knows that God is good. She delights in the morning, greets noonday scratching at the door to go out, and becomes especially wary when the sun goes down. She is the wild side of me, expressing *my life without* words. Somehow, she makes my playing with words more possible and more fulfilling. She and I have a perfect understanding about life. Language is good but language is not all there is. By sharing her domains of smells and sounds, I become more aware of the secret life that leads us.

"Every creature is a word of God," said Meister Eckehart, a fourteenth-century German mystical theologian. Listening to the animals, we hear the secrets of the universe. 🐾

Canine Crackups

Today I sniffed many
Doggie derrieres—and I celebrate
By kissing your face.

I lie belly-up
In the sunshine, happier than
You will ever be.

I lift my leg and
Anoint each bush. Hello, Spot—
Sniff this and weep.

Dig under fence—why?
Because it's there. Because it's
There. Because it's there.

Look in my eyes and
Deny it. No human could
Love you so much.

My owners' mood is
Romantic—I lie near their
Feet, expelling much gas.

My human is home!
I am so ecstatic I
Have made a puddle.

FAMILY TREE Dogs, as well as wolves and foxes, are descended from a weasel-size, tree-climbing carnivore called Miacis, which existed about 40 million years ago. Dogs were among the first animals domesticated by cavemen, and we have canine fossils dated as early as 10,000 B.C.

The dog we would recognize today first appeared in Eurasia about 13,000 years ago, and was probably directly descended from a small gray wolf—not from the jackal or jackal/wolf as previously thought. The greyhound is considered the most ancient dog breed, while the saluki is thought to have originated in ancient Mesopotamia around 3000 B.C. Irish wolfhounds trace their roots to 273 B.C. Ownership of these gigantic dogs was limited to emperors, kings, and the highest-ranking members of society, and they were held so dear that battles were fought over them. Roman consul Quintus Aurelius wrote of receiving no less than seven awe-inspiring wolfhounds as a gift in A.D. 391.

Canine Culture

A DOG'S LIFE Canine behavior may seem like so much licking, peeing, scratching, yipping, nipping, and sniffing, but dog society actually relies upon a complex system of rituals and behaviors. Spend an afternoon at the dog run to get a glimpse of the way dogs make friends and work in groups.

The gregarious wild-hunting-dog packs of Africa are a fascinating study in cooperative living. Only one dog in each pack can become the "alpha" female, who chooses the alpha male from among her suitors. Pairs generally remain monogamous for life! The pair is the only one in the pack allowed to mate: In their own form of Planned Parenthood, the other dogs suppress their breeding instinct, assuring that only the fittest in the pack reproduce. (If a subordinate female does give birth, she is usually met with violence, her pups often taken away by the alpha female.) The alpha male leads hunting forays. The dogs in the pack greet the alpha pair with the same groveling, licking, rolling, and tail-wagging gestures that our own dogs use to greet us! The alphas, in return, express a protective dominance by affectionately licking, pawing, or standing over their "subjects," just as bossy dogs do at the dog run. Living hierarchically is so important to dogs that hunting-dog packs as large as 100 animals have been recorded. To your pet at home, the "alpha dog" is you!

DOGGY DRIVES

All dogs possess a prey drive, defined as the urge to hunt, kill, and eat, which is modified to varying degrees by breeding and training. The first pack-hunting dogs were bred in China, and indeed, a great deal of the dog's early domestication took place here during ancient times. The prey drive is further evident in the frenetic herding behavior of the highly skilled Border collie, a "working breed" so loved as to inspire a television special. Dogs with a strong prey drive sometimes need to be "deprogrammed" not to chase cars, joggers, and bicyclists.

But Mom Didn't Like Dogs

by Dr. Donald R. Stoltz

We first met Chester, March second, 1965,
A shaggy, dirty bag of fur with big brown sorry eyes,
It was my sister's birthday, the day that she was eight,
When we saw him sitting in our yard, next to the garden gate.
We hurried out to pet him as fast as we could race,
And he almost had a smile on his straggly, lonely face.
But Mom didn't like dogs and said he couldn't stay,
And 'cause Mom didn't like dogs, she sent him on his way.

On April tenth of '65 we saw our friend again,
He was standing in the pouring rain outside the family den.
It was my father's birthday, and the house was full of guests;
So they really didn't miss us when we vanished from the rest.
We took a dish of ice cream and a piece of apple pie,
And when Father found us feeding Chet, a twinkle lit his eye.
But Mom didn't like dogs and said she was afraid,
And 'cause Mom didn't like dogs, she sent him on his way.

On June fifth of '65 it was birthday time again,
And Mom was having a party for the family
    and her friends.
When suddenly a commotion filled the summer air,
And there was Chester looking like a thrown-out
    teddy bear.
He looked so strange and funny, he made everybody laugh,
And Dad decided that our friend deserved a
    nice warm bath.
But Mom didn't like dogs—especially a stray,
And 'cause Mom didn't like dogs, she sent him on his way.

But by now we all were wondering and were really
    quite amazed
That Chester only seemed to come on very special days.
And when my birthday came around, the twelfth of that
    December,
I waited, watched, and wondered if Chester
    would remember.
By afternoon the heavy snows had piled up a drift

When through the storm I heard a bark, my special
    birthday gift.
But Mom didn't like dogs, so I pleaded and I prayed;
And though Mom didn't like dogs, she weakened,
    and he stayed.

Now many years have come and gone since 1965,
When we first met our dog, Chester, with the
    big brown sorry eyes.
And yesterday Pete, our postman, came and rang
    the back doorbell,
And told us he was retiring and had a tale to tell.
He told us he owned Chester, but back in '65,
He had to find a home for him after his wife died.
So each time we had a birthday and he delivered us a card,
He also would deliver Chester to our yard.
'Cause he knew how much we all loved dogs, and he knew
    that Mom would bend;
And although our mom never did like dogs,
    now Chester's her best friend.

Teaching the SIT

The Sit is perhaps the base for all good dog behavior. This simple trick will prove priceless in an infinite number of everyday dog situations. Some trainers use luring with food and some use a dog clicker to accomplish this task, while others use both.

1. If you hold a treat above the pup's head, she will automatically sit down as she looks up, and will earn that treat. Professional trainers often mark the exact moment when "the heinie hits the floor" with a sound to strengthen the behavior.
2. Whether you use a clicker, a clap, or your voice with the command "sit," be sure to reward your dog and praise effusively. Try to lengthen the time of the sit.
3. Reward the dog for holding the sit until you say "okay." By the way, there's no need for training a "sit-stay." Every sit is a sit-stay: The dog who learns the sit will sit until you release her with "okay." Dogs catch on to this game very, very fast.

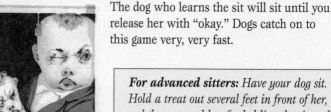

> **For *advanced sitters:*** *Have your dog sit. Hold a treat out several feet in front of her, and then reward her for holding the sit and not taking the treat until you say "okay." Don't try long holds at first; you must work up to it, or your dog will quit in frustration.*

Next to one's bosom friend, what companion like a dog? Your thought is his thought, your wish is his wish, and where you desire to go, that place of all others is preferable to him.

—JOHN BURROUGHS

Stickeen

by John Muir

But poor Stickeen, the wee, silky, sleekit beastie—think of him!
When I had decided to try the bridge, and while I was on my
knees cutting away the rounded brow, he came behind me,
pushed his head past my shoulder, looked down and across, scanned the
sliver and its approaches with his queer eyes, then looked me in the face
with a startled air of surprise and concern, and began to mutter and
whine, saying as plainly as if speaking with words, "Surely you are not
going to try that awful place?" This was the first time I had seen him
gaze deliberately into a crevasse or into my face with a speaking look.
That he should have recognized and appreciated the danger at the first
glance showed wonderful sagacity. Never before had the quick, daring
midget seemed to know that ice was slippery, or that there was such a
thing as danger anywhere. His looks and the tones of his voice when he
began to complain and speak his fears were so human that I uncon-
sciously talked to him as I would to a boy, and in trying to calm his fears
perhaps in some measure moderated my own. "Hush your fears, my
boy," I said, "we will get across safe, though it is not going to be easy.
No right way is easy in this rough world. We must risk our lives to save
theirs. At the worst we can only slip; and then how grand a grave we
shall have! And by and by our nice bones will do good in the terminal
moraine." But my sermon was far from reassuring him; he began to cry,
and after taking another piercing look at the tremendous gulf, ran away

in desperate excitement seeking some other crossing. By the time he got back, baffled, of course, I had made a step or two. I dared not look back, but he made himself heard; and when he saw that I was certainly crossing, he cried aloud in despair. The danger was enough to daunt anybody, but it seems wonderful that he should have been able to weigh and appreciate it so justly. No mountaineer could have seen it more quickly or judged it more wisely, discriminating between real and apparent peril.

After I had gained the other side he howled louder than ever, and after running back and forth in vain search for a way of escape, he would return to the brink of the crevasse above the bridge, moaning and groaning as if in the bitterness of death. Could this be the silent, philosophic Stickeen? I shouted encouragement, telling him the bridge was not so bad as it looked, that I had left it flat for his feet, and he could walk it easily. But he was afraid to try it. Strange that so small an animal should be capable of such big, wise fears! I called again and again in a reassuring tone to come on and fear nothing; that he could come if he would only try. Then he would hush for a moment, look again at the bridge, and shout his unshakable conviction that he could never, never come that way; then lie back in despair, as if howling: "Oh-o-o, what a place! No-o-o; I can never go-o-o down there!" His natural composure and courage had vanished utterly in a tumultuous storm of fear. Had the danger been less, his distress would have seemed ridiculous. But in this gulf—a huge, yawning sepulcher big enough to hold everybody in the territory—lay the shadow of death, and his heartrending cries might well have called Heaven to his help. Perhaps they did. So hidden before, he was transpar-

ent now, and one could see the workings of his mind like the movements
of a clock out of its case. His voice and gestures were perfectly human,
and his hopes and fears unmistakable, while he seemed to understand
every word of mine. I was troubled at the thought of leaving him. It
seemed impossible to get him to venture. To compel him to try by fear of
being left, I started off as if leaving him to his fate, and disappeared back
of a hummock; but this did no good, for he only lay down and cried. So
after hiding a few minutes, I went back to the brink of the crevasse, and
in a severe tone of voice shouted across to him that now I must certainly
leave him—I could wait no longer, and that if he would not come, all I
could promise was that I would return to seek him next day. I warned
him that if he went back to the woods the wolves would kill him, and
finished by urging him once more by words and gestures to come on. He
knew very well what I meant, and at last, with the courage of despair,
hushed and breathless, he lay down on the brink in
the hollow I had made for my knees, pressed his
body against the ice to get the advantage of the
friction, gazed into the first step, put his little
feet together, and slid them slowly down into it,
bunching all four in it, and almost standing on his
head. Then, without lifting them, as well as I could
see through the snow, he slowly worked them over the
edge of the step, and down into the next and the next in
succession in the same way, and gained the bridge. Then
lifting his feet with the regularity and slowness of the

273

vibrations of a seconds' pendulum, as if counting and measuring one, two, three, holding himself in dainty poise, and giving separate attention to each little step, he gained the foot of the cliff, at the top of which I was kneeling to give him a lift should he get within reach. Here he halted in dead silence, and it was here I feared he might fail, for dogs are poor climbers. I had no cord. If I had had one, I would have dropped a noose over his head and hauled him up. But while I was thinking whether an available cord might be made out of clothing, he was looking keenly into the series of notched steps and finger-holds of the ice-ladder I had made, as if counting them and fixing the position of each one in his mind. Then suddenly up he came, with a nervy, springy rush, hooking his paws into the notches and steps so quickly that I could not see how it was done, and whizzed past my head, safe at last!

And now came a scene! "Well done, well done, little boy! Brave boy!" I cried, trying to catch and caress him; but he would not be caught. Never before or since have I seen anything like so passionate a revulsion from the depths of despair to uncontrollable, exultant, triumphant joy. He flashed and darted hither and thither as if fairly demented, screaming and shouting, swirling round and round in giddy loops and circles like a leaf in a whirlwind, lying down and rolling over and over, sidewise and heels over head, pouring forth a tumultuous flood of hysterical cries and sobs and gasping mutterings. And when I ran up to him to shake him, fearing he might die of joy, he flashed off two or three hundred yards, his feet in a mist of motion; then, turning suddenly, he came back in wild rushes, and launched himself at my face, almost knocking me down, all the time screeching and screaming and shouting as if saying, "Saved! saved! saved! Then away again, dropping suddenly at times with his feet in the air, trembling, and fairly sobbing. Such passionate emotion was enough to kill him. Who could have guessed the capacity of the dull, enduring little fellow for all that most stirs this mortal frame? Nobody could have helped crying with him.

But there is nothing like work for toning down either excessive fear or joy. So I ran ahead, calling him, in as gruff a voice as I could command, to come on and stop his nonsense, for we had far to go, and it would soon be dark. Neither of us feared another trial like this. Heaven would surely count one enough for a lifetime. The ice ahead was gashed by thousands of crevasses, but they were common ones. The joy of deliverance burned in us like fire, and we ran without fatigue, every muscle, with immense rebound, glorying in its strength. Stickeen flew across everything in his way, and not till dark did he settle into his normal fox-like, gliding trot. At last the mountains crowned with spruce came in sight, looming faintly in the gloaming, and we soon felt the solid rock beneath our feet, and were safe. Then came weariness. We stumbled down along the lateral moraine in the dark, over rocks and tree-trunks, through the bushes and devil-club thickets and mossy logs and boulders of the woods where we had sheltered ourselves in the morning. Then out on the level mud-slope of the terminal moraine. Danger had vanished, and so had our strength. We reached camp about ten o'clock, and found a big fire and a big supper. A party of Hoona Indians had visited Mr. Young, bringing a gift of porpoise-meat and wild strawberries, and hunter Joe had brought in a wild goat. But we lay down, too tired to eat mush, and soon fell into a troubled sleep. The man who said, "The harder the toil the sweeter the rest," never was profoundly tired. Stickeen kept springing up and muttering in his sleep, no doubt dreaming that he was still on the brink of the crevasse; and so did I—that night and many others, long afterward, when I was nervous and overtired.

Thereafter Stickeen was a changed dog. During the rest of the trip, instead of holding aloof, he would come to me at night when all was quiet about the camp-fire, and rest his head on my knee, with a look of devotion, as if I were his god. And often, as he caught my eye, he seemed to be trying to say, "Wasn't that an awful time we had together on the glacier?" 🐾

Rin Tin Tin

Rin Tin Tin first appeared as a talented German shepherd devastated by war, but he would inspire a famous lineage that continues today. On September 15, 1918, Corporal Lee Duncan and his battalion investigated a bombed-out dog kennel in Lorraine, France, and discovered the only survivors—a female German shepherd and her litter of five puppies. Duncan kept two pups, one of each gender, for himself and left the others in the care of the battalion. Unfortunately, the rest of the litter perished in the war, but Duncan's puppies survived. He was so astonished at the abilities of the shepherds that he visited the captured German kennel master in the prison camp to learn more about the breed. When Duncan returned to the United States following the war, the female shepherd, Nanette, became ill and died. Duncan had met a noted shepherd breeder who had tried to help him restore Nanette to health. The breeder understood Duncan's passion for German shepherds and replaced the deceased pup with another fine female. The male, whom Duncan named Rin Tin Tin, lived to develop many amazing abilities. At a 1922 dog show, Rin Tin Tin impressed spectators by jumping 13½ feet, and it was caught on film. Duncan pursued Rin Tin Tin's movie career with energy and determination despite being initially shut out by show business. The pair ultimately landed 26 movie deals with Warner Brothers, and the films' success saved the studio from financial ruin. When Rin Tin Tin passed away, Duncan selected a puppy, named Junior, from one of Rin Tin Tin's several litters and toured America. Junior won the hearts and minds of fans across the nation and also became the first dog in history to make a commercial airplane flight. Rin Tin Tin III, Junior's half-brother, later assisted Duncan in establishing a war-dog school at Camp Hahn, training over 5,000 dogs and handlers for WWII efforts. Convinced that the German shepherd breed could achieve even greater excellence, Duncan expanded the Rin Tin Tin name to another fine shepherd bloodline, producing Rin Tin Tin II who costarred with Rin Tin Tin IV in the ABC series *The Adventures of Rin Tin Tin* from 1954 to 1959. With the help of Jannettia Brodsgaard Propps and her granddaughter, Daphne Hereford, this second and final Rin Tin Tin bloodline continues to the present day even after Duncan's 1960 death. 🐾

Fetch!

Some dogs are natural retreivers, bringing "presents" until they drive their owners crazy, and other dogs simply will not learn to fetch, grabbing the object and running away with it every time. This game works best if your dog has some experience with Take It and Leave It (p. 320). Amateur trainers often think that the retrieve is one of the most frustrating things to teach. To teach it correctly, you must start at the "tail end" of the game, with the part you want last. That is, you want your dog to give the object to you.

1. Have your dog sit. Place a stick or other object in front of her. When she picks it up, hold one hand out and hold a treat in the other hand. Treat her as soon as she relinquishes it. Add the cue "Fetch!" Do a series of 20 or so repetitions of this, until you are going at lightning-fast speed. Your dog is having a ball!

2. "Backchain" the retrieve: Toss the object only a couple of feet away and hold out your hand very broadly as a visual cue. Say "Fetch." In your other hand, hold a treat. Just stand there—don't move, chase her, or grab at her. If she teases you or runs away with the object say "Ahhh-ah!" in disgust, turn your back, and walk away. She'll probably follow you. If she brings it but only wants to play tug of war, follow the directions in Leave It (p. 321).

3. Continue to ask for the object with the cue, holding out your hand without moving, until she surrenders it or drops it at your feet. Huge treat!

4. Repeat the exercise, gradually lengthening the distance you toss the object by very small increments. Backtrack to step one whenever the dog "slips up." Some natural retrievers will catch on immediately.

Beautiful Joe

by Marshall Saunders

Mr. Wood called October the golden month. Everything was quiet and still, and at night and in the mornings the sun had a yellow, misty look. The trees in the orchard were loaded with fruit, and some of the leaves were floating down, making a soft covering on the ground.

In the garden there were a great many flowers in bloom, in flaming red and yellow colors. Miss Laura gathered bunches of them every day to put in the parlor. One day when she was arranging them, she said regretfully: "They will soon be gone. I wish it could always be summer."

"You would get tired of it," said Mr. Harry, who had come up softly behind her. "There's only one place where we could stand perpetual summer, and that's in heaven."

"Do you suppose that it will always be summer there?" said Miss Laura, turning around and looking at him.

"I don't know. I imagine it will be, but I don't think anybody knows much about it. We've got to wait."

Miss Laura's eyes fell on me. "Harry," she said, "do you think that dumb animals will go to heaven?"

"I shall have to say again, I don't know," he replied. "Some people hold that they do. In a Michigan paper, the other day, I came across one writer's opinion on the subject. He says that among the best people of all ages have been some who believed in the future life of animals. Homer and the later Greeks, some of the Romans and early Christians held this view—the last believing that God sent angels in the shape of birds to comfort sufferers for the faith. Saint Francis called the birds and beasts his brothers. Doctor Johnson believed in a future life for animals, as also did Wordsworth, Shelley, Coleridge, Jeremy Taylor, Agassiz, Lamartine, and many Christian scholars. It seems as if they ought to have some compensation for their terrible sufferings in this world. Then to go to heaven, animals would only have to take up the thread of their lives here. Man is a god to the lower creation. Joe worships you, much as you worship your Maker. Dumb animals live in and for their masters. They hand on our words and looks, and are dependent on us in almost every way. For my own part, and looking at it from an earthly point of view, I wish with all my heart that we may find our dumb friends in paradise."

"And in the Bible," said Miss Laura, "animals are often spoken of. The dove and the raven, the wolf and the lamb, and the leopard, and the cattle that God says are His, and the little sparrow that can't fall to the ground without our Father's knowing it."

"Still there's nothing definite about their immortality,"

said Mr. Harry. "However, we have nothing to do with that. If it's right for them to be in heaven, we'll find them there. All we have to do now is to deal with the present, and the Bible plainly tells us that 'a righteous man regardeth the life of his beast.'"

"I think I should be happier in heaven if dear old Joe were there," said Miss Laura, looking wistfully at me. "He has been such a good dog. Just think how he has loved and protected me. I think I should be lonely without him."

"That reminds me of some poetry, or rather doggerel," said Mr. Harry, "that I cut out of a newspaper for you yesterday," and he drew from his pocket a little slip of paper, and read this:

> "Do doggies gang to heaven, Dad?
> Will oor auld Donald gang?
> For noo to tak' him, faither, wi' us,
> Wad be maist awfu' wrang."

There were other verses, telling how many kind things old Donald the dog had done for his master's family, and then it closed with these lines:

> "Withoot are dogs. Eh, faither, man,
> 'Twould be an awfu' sin

283

To leave oor faithfu' doggie there,
He's certain to win in.
"Oor Donald's no like ither dogs,
He'll no be locket oot,
If Donald's no let into heaven,
I'll no gang there one foot."

"My sentiments exactly," said a merry voice behind Miss
Laura and Mr. Harry, and looking up they saw Mr.
Maxwell. He was holding out one hand to them, and in the
other kept back a basket of large pears that Mr. Harry
promptly took from him, and offered to Miss Laura. "I've
been dependent upon animals for the most part of my comfort in this life," said Mr. Maxwell, "and I sha'n't be happy
without them in heaven. I don't see how you would get on
without Joe, Miss Morris, and I want my birds, and my
snake, and my horse—how can I live without them? They're
almost all my life here."

"If some animals go to heaven and not others, I think that
the dog has the first claim," said Miss Laura. "He's the
friend of man—the oldest and best. Have you ever heard the
legend about him and Adam?"

"No," said Mr. Maxwell.

"Well, when Adam was turned out of paradise, all the animals shunned him, and he sat weeping bitterly with his

284

head between his hands, when he felt the soft tongue of some creature gently touching him. He took his hands from his face, and there was a dog that had separated himself from all the other animals, and was trying to comfort him. He became the chosen friend and companion of Adam, and afterward of all men."

"There is another legend," said Mr. Harry, "about our Saviour and a dog. Have you ever heard it?"

"We'll tell you that later," said Mr. Maxwell, "when we know what it is."

Mr. Harry showed his white teeth in an amused smile, and began: "Once upon a time our Lord was going through a town with his disciples. A dead dog lay by the wayside, and every one that passed along flung some offensive epithet at him. Eastern dogs are not like our dogs, and seemingly there was nothing good about this loathsome creature, but as our Saviour went by, he said, gently, 'Pearls cannot equal the whiteness of his teeth.'"

"What was the name of that old fellow," said Mr. Maxwell abruptly, "who had a beautiful swan that came every day for fifteen years, to bury its head in his bosom and feed from his hand, and would go near no other human being?"

"Saint Hugh, of Lincoln. We heard about him at the Band of Mercy the other day," said Miss Laura.

"I should think that he would have wanted to have that swan in heaven with him," said Mr. Maxwell. "What a beautiful creature it must have been. Speaking about animals going to heaven, I dare say some of them would object to going, on account of the company they would meet there. Think of the dog kicked to death by his master, the horse driven into his grave, the thousands of cattle starved to death on the plains—will they want to meet their owners in heaven?"

"According to my reckoning, their owners won't be there," said Mr. Harry. "I firmly believe that the Lord will punish every man or woman who ill-treats a dumb creature, just as surely as he will punish those who ill-treat their fellow creatures. If a man's life has been a long series of cruelty to dumb animals, do you suppose that he would enjoy himself in heaven, which will be full of kindness to every one? Not he, he'd rather be in the other place, and there he'll go, I fully believe."

"When you've quite disposed of all your fellow creatures and the dumb creation, Harry, perhaps you will condescend to go out in the orchard and see how your father is getting on with picking the apples," said Mrs. Wood, joining Laura and the two young men, her eyes twinkling and sparkling with amusement.

"The apples will keep, mother," said Mr. Harry, putting his arm around her. "I just came in for a moment to get Laura. Come, Maxwell, we'll all go."

"And not another word about animals," Mrs. Wood called after them. "Laura will go crazy some day, through thinking of their sufferings, if some one doesn't do something to stop her."

Miss Laura turned around suddenly. "Dear Aunt Hattie," she said, "you must not say that. I am a coward, I know, about hearing of animals' pains, but I must get over it. I want to know how they suffer. I ought to know, for when I get to be a woman, I am going to do all I can to help them."

"And I'll join you," said Mr. Maxwell, stretching out his hand to Miss Laura. She did not smile, but looking very earnestly at him, she held it clasped in her own. "You will help me care for them, will you?" she said.

"Yes, I promise," he said gravely. "I'll give myself to the service of dumb animals, if you will."

"And I too," said Mr. Harry, in his deep voice, laying his hand across theirs. Mrs. Wood stood looking at their three fresh, eager young faces with tears in her eyes. Just as they all stood silently for an instant, the old village clergyman came into the room from the hall. He must have heard what they said, for before they could move he had laid his hands on their three brown heads. "Bless you, my children," he said, "God will lift up the light of his countenance upon you, for you have given yourselves to a noble work. In serving dumb creatures, you are ennobling the human race."

What dogs are best for sending telegrams?

Wire-haired terriers.

What do you call a happy Lassie?

A jolly collie.

What do you call a nutty dog in Australia?

A dingo-ling.

What happens when it rains cats and dogs?

You may step in a poodle.

What kind of dog does Dracula have?

A bloodhound.

What did the hungry Dalmatian say
when he ate his lunch?

That hit the spots.

What dog wears contact lenses?

A cockeyed spaniel.

What do you get if you cross a
sheepdog with a rose?

A collie flower.

What
dog
loves
to take
bubble
baths?

A shampoodle.

WHY DO DOGS CHASE CARS? Chasing cars, Frisbees, kids on bikes, joggers, and even cats are outlets for the prey drive. Prey drive in pet dogs often expresses itself as a game of "doggy tag," in which participants take turns being "it." Dogs may snap playfully or "lunge" at one another during the chase. The object isn't really to catch the other dog or the car but simply to run around and let off steam.

Some dogs will, however, attempt to catch and subdue the object of the chase. Sporting dogs, herding dogs, terriers, and hounds have an enhanced prey drive. Behavior in which a dog chases, hunts down, and tries to wound or kill is predatory aggression, which is normal dog behavior, not a disorder. If your dog displays predatory aggression, you should supervise her at all times and not let her run loose where she could hurt someone.

Dog FAQs

WHY DO DOGS TURN AROUND AND AROUND BEFORE LYING DOWN? Behaviorists say this is an instinctive nesting behavior, done to "flatten the grass" and make a comfy spot for a nap. Hounds and oudoor-type dogs especially will do this.

DO DOGS HAVE EMOTIONS? In 350 B.C., Aristotle wrote, in History of Animals, "Some are good-tempered, sluggish, and little prone to ferocity, as the ox; others are quick-tempered, ferocious, and unteachable, as the wild boar." Many owners and researchers assert that there's no reason to think that dogs don't have feelings.

CAN DOGS LEARN WORDS? Dogs are attuned to sounds humans make, but they are much better than we previously thought at understanding visual signals. A perfect example is the deaf Dalmatian named Hogan who knows 45 words in American Sign Language.

DO DOGS SEE COLOR? The common belief that dogs are completely colorblind is false. Dogs can see color, but not as vividly as we do. It is much like our vision at twilight.

WHY DO DOGS CHASE THEIR TAILS?

This is one of the activities that actually helps build paw-eye (or in this case, tail-eye) coordination, a necessary faculty for hunting. If your dog does this obsessively, however, it may be a sign of boredom, anxiety, or a nervous disorder.

GOOD LUCK

Meditatio

By Ezra Pound

When I carefully
   consider the curious
   habits of dogs
I am compelled to
   conclude
That man *is* the
   superior animal.

When I consider
   the curious habits
   of man
I confess, my friend,
   I am puzzled.

Teaching the HEEL

Having a dog who heels is a joy. You can even train your dog to heel off leash.

Start indoors, preferably while the dog is still less than 5 months old, and resist the urge to tighten or yank on the leash. Make sure you keep it slack.

One way of training the heel is to stop and stand still when your dog pulls out ahead against your wishes, to let him know that the walk won't resume until he's ready to walk next to you. A Gentle Leader Headcollar, available from various online retailers, is recommended.

Motivate your pooch to walk next to you by carrying a big bag of kibble or treats every time you go out. Capitalize on the power of positive association by using food as a lure to get your dog to keep his head near your knee. Rewarding the dog on a slack leash causes him to heel because he wants to and not because you are threatening him with hauling him back by his neck with a choker collar.

Teaching the heel is one activity many owners find easier through the use of a clicker or other sound, especially for an adult dog. If you don't have a way to mark the instant your dog moves into the correct position, you can run the risk of making harsh corrections out of frustration over not being able to com-

municate with the dog. Once he understands what you are asking for, you won't need the clicker anymore. Some clicker trainers don't use the leash at all when teaching the heel—we watched one train a puppy to heel in 10 minutes.

Whatever tools you choose, as with other training tasks, add the cue, "Heel" when your dog seems to be getting it.

My little dog—a heartbeat at my feet. —EDITH WHARTON

Fred, A Dog Gone But Not Forgotten

by Thomas M. Boyd

During his life, which I think was a good one even by canine standards, Fred saw his role change from that of a nonpaying roommate to the surrogate child of newlyweds to the elder statesman of a growing family of five—counting Fred. Brooke, my seven-year-old daughter, first met him when he poked his moist, collie nose into her bassinet and introduced himself with an impromptu lick. My 16-month-old son received the same initiation when he joined the family.

Brooke learned to walk partly because of Fred—or Fef, or Fud, or Ferd, depending on her stage of vocal aptitude at the time. He became the prop against which she leaned when she tried to stand, and he stoically held his ground when she mercilessly tugged on his black and white coat in her first attempts to walk. He even taught her respect for traffic; whenever I instructed him to sit at intersections, she would watch him carefully and squat. ❧

Patches' Devotion

On a cold winter night in December 1965, a collie/malamute mix named Patches displayed uncanny strength, loyalty, and heroism in the rescue of his master, Marvin Scott, from the icy water of Lake Spanaway in Spanaway, Washington. With the temperature holding well below freezing and the lake water churning violently from the cold wind, Patches accompanied Scott to the pier to check a patrol boat for ice damage. As Scott pulled the stern line to free his boat from the frozen lake's surface, he slipped and fell from the icy pier onto the floating dock below, tearing muscles and tendons in both of his legs. Then he slid into the freezing water. Patches immediately dove into the water and began tugging Scott by his hair to the edge of the floating dock. Through the haze of half-consciousness, Scott realized the dog's predicament and lifted Patches onto the dock. Scott was unable to save himself with his injuries, however, and sunk back into the black lake water. Patches leapt in and made another rescue attempt, but again Scott was too exhausted to lift himself to safety. Scott screamed for help, but his cries were swept away by the winter gusts. The situation appeared hopeless, and Scott had depleted all his remaining energy in the struggle.

Even in the delirium caused by the trauma, he understood that death was imminent, and he accepted his fate, sinking into the water a final time. But Patches would not give up, and pulled Scott up by the collar, and through a combination of their efforts, they struggled from the water. As Patches kept a grip on his collar, Scott crawled on his elbows up the rocky 300-foot incline, where he managed to attract his wife's attention by throwing stones.

For the next 25 days, Scott underwent numerous operations and barely eluded death. During his recovery, Scott required the use of two canes for walking, and Patches, who had fully recovered, would slow his pace to match that of his master's when they continued their regular walks around the lake.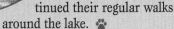

Puppy Push-Ups

A universal favorite among animal trainers and a crowd pleaser among guests, Push-Ups combine numerous commands into a complex and entertaining new trick.

1. First, prime your pup by teaching him the sit and the down. Some people do this by luring with treats and rewarding the dog when he has done it right, and some add the sound of a dog clicker or other noise. Either way, you will be rewarding your dog with food and praise. Reward your dog for a sit (p. 264). Then wiggle a treat in front of your sitting dog and move your hand to floor level with the treat held under it. As your pooch tries to investigate under your hand with her nose, she will probably lower her body to the floor. This is the perfect opportunity for you to "capture" the down. Say "Good!" and give her a treat.

2. Do it again, adding the cue "Down." Now "pull" the pup back up with another treat, saying "Sit." Repeat the Push-Up a number of times, alternating between the sit and the down. Gradually do less luring with food and more asking for the behaviors with your voice.

3. The next time you have a gathering of children or friends, have them sit in a circle on the floor with the dog in the middle. Demonstrate the Push-Up with your pup. Have players take turns, each of them asking him to do three Push-Ups in succession. Each time he does it right, say "Good!" and treat; each time he doesn't, make a different sound, like "Uh-oh!" and repeat the cue.

4. If your pup is too excited or distracted to focus on what the group wants, treat him anyway and try a simpler behavior, like the Recall Game (p.155).

#86 by Lawrence Ferlinghetti

The dog hangs his snout
    out the auto window
Too long city-pent
   his nose is out for wild game
His tongue hangs out
    when he gets the scent
    of small creatures in the underbrush
for whom every car is a brush
    with disaster
And the dog feels for them
   with his so sad eyes
but looks at them
    through the eyes of his master

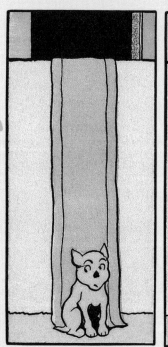
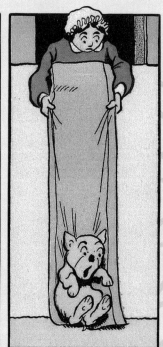

Canine Crackups

What is a dog's artistic medium?

Nose prints

Why do dogs wag their tails?

Because no one else will do it for them!

Why didn't the dog speak to his foot?

Because it's not polite to talk back to your paw!

What is the dog's favorite city?

New Yorkie!

Who is the dog's favorite comedian?

Growlcho Marx!

What did the cowboy say when the bear ate Lassie?

"Well, doggone!"

What happened when the dog went to the flea circus?

He stole the show!

Why did the cowboy get a dachsund?

His boss told him to get a long, little doggie.

Why did the poor dog chase his own tail?

He was trying to make both ends meet!

HAIR CARE Longhaired dogs need several brushings per week, while even short-coated canines will appreciate a regular brushing or rubdown with a rubber mitt, and ear and eye cleaning. There exists a vast array of specialized shedding tools and mat combs for the home groomer. Choose finer-toothed combs for silky hair, coarse-toothed ones for heavy coats. It may take several grooming sessions to get through mats. Do not attempt to cut out mats with scissors unless the dog is restrained; you can cut the dog's skin.

DOGGY 'DO'S You've might have heard of the spaniel cut, the lion cut, the terrier cut. Before you attempt any fancy "doggy 'do's," invest in a good pair of clippers, an appropriate brush, and a book or video on doggy coiffure. Better yet, leave the fine work to a groomer recommended by your vet. Experts say, however, that when a pup receives grooming and trimming at

From Head to Tail
Grooming Your Dog

home, his first trip to the salon is more likely to be a pleasant one. And you are more likely to be satisfied if you can precisely describe the style you want.

HEAD It's a myth that longhaired dogs must have their eyes shaded; they see fine when all that hair is pulled up or trimmed away! Your vet can look with a flashlight for common problems, such as eyelid hair or inward-rolling lids, that might irritate the cornea and cause excessive tearing. Clean away eye stains and crusting with sterile saline. Regular trimming of excess eyelid hair helps keep tear ducts clear. You or your groomer should be especially careful in using clippers around the face, as clipper burns or "hot spots" are most common in these areas. Tiny nicks will drive your dog crazy, and may even require antibiotic treatment. If you see your dog scratching at his head or body a few days after clipping, have a vet inspect the area.

Shaving ear hairs can be beneficial in preventing inflamed ears, or otitis. The trimming blade must be kept flat and not at an angle to the skin. As for plucking, it's best to leave this to a knowledgeable groomer, since it can make some ear conditions worse.

TOES Not all dogs will need nail trimming, but they do if they don't have the opportunity to wear them down naturally. Use a trimmer with a guillotine-type blade (or a claw cutter for large breeds), have styptic powder on hand, and have your vet show you how the first time. Try not to force your dog by grabbing and squeezing the feet too hard. If she likes to relax by rolling on her back, you can use this time for grooming. Practice by cutting the end of a nail from underneath. Remember to reward your pooch with her favorite treat for cooperating! If your dog is well behaved, this is a good time to trim hair from paw pads with clippers, if needed.

TAIL Finally, some dogs' bathroom habits might dictate some detail work with the clippers to help keep this area neat and clean.

The Hairy Dog
by Herbert Asquith

My dog's so furry I've not seen
His face for years and years;
His eyes are buried out of sight,
I only guess his ears.

When people ask me for his breed,
I do not know or care;
He has the beauty of them all
Hidden beneath his hair.

313

Bathtime!

Your local pet store and the Internet are filled with dog shampoos for every taste—primarily marketed to appeal to humans and their pocketbooks. Just be sure to use a veterinarian-recommended formula. Your dog may not appreciate a lot of the perfumes we humans do; these in fact can be overpowering to a sensitive nose.

"Stinky Dog" Syndrome

The reasons for foul odor include rolling in something bad-smelling (some dogs regard this as perfume), being sprayed by a skunk, infected ears or anal glands, or other conditions. Do not attempt to treat undiagnosed problems with shampoo.

Itchy Infestations

If your pet is scratching, has inflamed skin, or you think fleas might be a problem, consult your vet before initiating treament. Don't depend on shampoos for complete flea control. Discuss with your vet the use of medications, collars, and environmental control.

How to Give a Dog a Bath

1. Use lukewarm water; human baths are too warm.
2. Enlist an assistant to lovingly embrace and encourage a worrisome pooch. Or place the dog in the tub prior to filling it, allowing her to adjust.
3. Wet the neck area thoroughly and lather with shampoo. This acts as a barrier to fleas that will try to escape to the face and ears.
4. Now wet the body and lather well. If possible, try to let the shampoo sit for a few minutes. Rinse well.
5. Follow up with a good conditioner.
6. Have on hand a couple of big fluffy towels for doggy drying. If you must use a hair dryer, as with a longhaired dog, use a no-heat, low setting only: Dogs' skin is very easily overheated and dried out.

Talkin' 'bout the Dog Wash

Ever think you'd see the day when you could go to the self-serve dog wash down the block and "Simonize" your pooch? Well, you can. A craze that started on the West Coast, these are actual places where you can hose down your dog at a professional grooming station and create your own canine makeover. Three of note are California's South Bark Dog Wash in San Diego and Canine Creek in Tehachapi, and the Dog Wash in New York City.

Have a "need to knead," and a four-legged food vacuum? Peanut butter is an all-time dog favorite—and nutritious too. But before trying out any new dog treats, be sure to get your vet's okay, especially if your pooch is on a special diet. Here's a healthy snack that's sure to tickle Toto's tongue.

1 cup peanut butter (with no added salt, sugar, or preservatives)
1/4 cup honey
2 cups low-sodium chicken broth
1/3 cup peanut oil
1 cup rolled oats
1 cup oat bran
3 1/2 to 4 cups oat flour

1. Preheat oven to 350°F.

2. In a large saucepan over medium-low heat, combine peanut butter, honey, chicken broth, and peanut oil. Heat to the simmering point, stirring frequently.

3. Remove from heat and stir in rolled oats and oat bran.

4. When cool enough to handle, add enough oat flour with your hands to form a stiff dough. Place on a floured surface and knead for several minutes until smooth.

5. Form the dough into a ball. Using a rolling pin, roll it out on the floured surface until you have a sheet about 1/4 inch thick. Cut into squares (or use cookie cutters if you prefer) and place on ungreased baking sheets about 1/2 inch apart.

6. Bake for a half hour, turn, and bake another half hour, or until golden brown. Refrigerate in an airtight container for up to 2 weeks, or freeze indefinitely.

Makes several dozen treats

Peanut Butter Biscuits

Russian Space Dogs

Space. The Final Frontier. To boldly go where no . . . dog . . . has gone before? That's right, the first living being shot into space was not a human, but a dog. And not merely one dog, but a long line of fearless Russian mutts helped determine if human spaceflight was feasible.

During the 1950s and 1960s, the Russian Space Agency launched some 26 dogs, a few multiple times, in suborbital and orbital flights as a means of testing the effects of prolonged weightlessness. Before becoming a cosmonaut, each of the Russian Space Dogs was a stray from the streets of Moscow. The scientists chose dogs over monkeys, who were thought to be too fidgety, and selected female canines because they had milder temperaments and were easier to clean up after than their male counterparts.

Dezik and Tsygan were the first dogs to make a suborbital flight on July 22, 1951. Both dogs were recovered unharmed after traveling to an altitude of 100 kilometers. Researchers launched several more dogs in suborbital flights in the subsequent years until orbital flights commenced.

Perhaps the most famous Russian Space Dog was Laika, meaning "barker," who is considered the first living being to enter outer space. On

November 3, 1957, Laika boarded Sputnik II, a 4-meter-high cone-shaped capsule carrying equipment and a small compartment for the dog that launched out of the atmosphere and into orbit around the Earth. Rocket engineers intended Laika to orbit for 10 days, but the capsule was not designed for a safe homecoming. After much controversy over how long she lived during the mission, they determined she passed away within several hours of the launch, likely from the harsh and unpredictable conditions of space travel.

The Space Agency skyrocketed more Space Dogs on orbital missions in the following years—losing some in flight, successfully bringing other dog-heroes back to Earth. One of these returning pooches, Strelka, gave birth to several puppies, one of whom was given to Caroline Kennedy, daughter of President John F. Kennedy. These courageous canines paved the way for subsequent primate and human missions. Without them, space programs throughout the world would not be what they are today. 🐾

Teaching TAKE IT and LEAVE IT

These exercises help to control an annoyingly mouthy, grabby pup. Once your pooch has these behaviors on cue, you can say "Leave it!" whenever he acts out with his mouth, whether it be snapping at pantlegs, mutilating your shoes, eating rocks, or chomping down on the TV remote. If you practice these exercises regularly and give your dog enough attention, he will lose interest in destroying forbidden belongings.

TAKE IT

1. Use a mouthable object, such as a floppy rubber toy, old towel, or stuffed animal, other than your dog's normal playthings. Wiggle it in front of him until he mouths it, and when he does, offer a treat and praise. Some trainers use the sound of a clicker. Whatever tool you use, be sure to reward your pup! When he gets it (dog trainers call this *startling*), you will see his eyes and ears perk up in response to you.

2. Start adding the cue, saying "Take it!" just before he picks it up. Give him two treats if he holds it for a second.

3. Support good mouthing behavior by showing him Kongs and other appropriate things to chew on. "Take it!" Treat!

LEAVE IT

How do you get the object back if your dog won't let go? The Leave It cue is an important way for you to keep your dog from picking up undesirable objects.

1. Let your dog grab the object. Say "Leave it," and hold on to it limply. Don't waggle or tug; it will encourage him to do the same. If he tugs, just let your hand go limply with it.
2. The second he lets go, pay him with a treat. If he continues his hold, distract him with a treat in your other hand. If he still won't let go, repeat the cue and blow in his nose. (For *extremely* mouthy, destructive dogs, you may have to resort to blocking his nostrils with the towel or stuffed toy for a second.) Treat, and repeat.
3. Practice "Leave it!" whenever he goes near your forbidden pillows, shoes, and other items, and give him a treat each time. Remember the adage "You catch more flies with honey than vinegar." It's better to reward him for dropping a forbidden object than it is to swat him for picking it up.

"Zen Doggy" version for advanced Takers and Leavers: Use the treat as the object. Have him sit or lie down, and hold the treat out in front of him for a few seconds before you say "Take it." Withdraw the treat if he approaches before you give the cue, putting him back in position and slowly extending the treat again. Once your dog gets it, you can even advance to placing a biscuit on his head! Do this in baby steps, or your dog will get discouraged.

Brownie

by T. H. White

Doolistown, Eire
November 25th, 1944

Dearest Bunny,

Brownie died today. In all her 14 years of life I have only been away from her at night for 3 times, once to visit England for 5 days, once to have my appendix out and once for tonsils (2 days), but I did go into Dublin about twice a year to buy books (9 hours away) and I thought she understood about this. Today I went at 10, but the bloody devils had managed to kill her somehow when I got back at 7. She was in perfect health. I left her in my bed this morning, as it was an early start. Now I am writing with her dead head in my lap. I will sit up with her tonight, but tomorrow we must bury her. I don't know what to do after that. I am only sitting up because of that thing about perhaps consciousness persisting a bit. She had been to me more perfect than anything else in all my life, and I have failed her at the end, an 180–1 chance. If it had been any other day I might have known that I had done my best. These fools here did not poison her—I will not believe that. But I could have done more. They kept rubbing her, they say. She looks quite alive. She was wife, mother, mistress & child. Please forgive me for writing this distressing stuff, but it is helping me. Her little

tired face cannot be helped. Please do not write to me at all
about her, for very long time, but tell me if I ought to buy
another bitch or not, as I do not know what to think about anything. I am certain I am not going to kill myself about it, as I
thought I might once. However, you will find this all very hysterical, so I may as well stop. I still expect to wake up and find it
wasn't. She was all I had.

    love from TIM

~

Doolistown
November 28th 1944

Dear Bunny,

Please forgive me writing again, but I am so lonely and
can't stop crying and it is the shock. I waked her for two
nights and buried her this morning in a turf basket, all my
eggs in one basket. Now I am to begin a new life and it is important to begin it right, but I find it difficult to think straight. It is
about whether I ought to buy another dog or not. I am good to
dogs, so from their point of view I suppose I ought. But I might
not survive another bereavement like this in 12 years' time, and
dread to put myself in the way of it. If your father & mother &
both sons had died at the same moment as Ray, unexpectedly, in
your absence, you would know what I am talking about.
Unfortunately Brownie was barren, like myself, and as I have

rather an overbearing character I had made her live through me, as I lived through her. Brownie was my life and I am lonely for just such another reservoir for my love. But if I did get such a reservoir it would die in about 12 years and at present I feel I couldn't face that. Do people get used to being bereaved? This is my first time. I am feeling very lucky to have a friend like you that I can write to without being thought dotty to go on like that about mere dogs.

They did not poison her. It was one of her little heart attacks and they did not know how to treat it and killed her by the wrong kindnesses.

You must try to understand that I am and will remain entirely without wife or brother or sister or child and that Brownie supplied more than the place of these to me. We loved each other more and more every year.

~

Doolistown
December 1944

Dear Bunny,

I am over the worst, though there is still one thing I can hardly bear to think of. Brownie had immense confidence in me as a doctor and used to come to me for help when she felt an attack coming on. She used to come and look up at me and register being ill. Because I was away, she couldn't do it when she

was dying, but she knew she was dying, and went to tell Mrs.
McDonagh as a last resource, which failed her. When I think of
this my heart is an empty funnel. There is a physical feeling in
it. After she was buried I stayed with the grave for one week, so
that I could go out twice a day and say 'Good girl: sleepy girl: go
to sleep, Brownie.' It was a saying she understood. I said it
steadily. I suppose the chance of consciousness persisting for a
week is several million to one, but that was the kind of chance I
had to provide against. She depended on me too much, and so I
had to accept too much responsibility for her. Then I went to
Dublin, against my will, and kept myself as drunk as possible for
nine days, and came back feeling more alive than dead. She was
the only wonderful thing that has happened to me, and presum-
ably the last one. You are wrong that her infertility was due to
our relationship. It was the other way round. She adopted me
off her own bat, and I took her to the sire at 18 months and several times after, before I cared two straws about her. I also took
her to vets, to find out why she flinched at the critical moment,
and they said that the passage was malformed. After that, I just
used to leave her loose when she was in season. I don't know
what I told you before, but I have found out some things. One is
that bereaved suicides commit it out of tidiness, not out of grand
emotions. Their habits, customs and interests, which means
their lives, were bound up with their loved one, so, when that
dies, they realize that their own habits etc. are dead. So, as they
see that they are dead already, they commit suicide in order to

be consistent. Everything is dead except their bodies, so they kill these too, to be tidy, like washing up after a meal or throwing away the empties after a party, and I daresay they find it as tedious. The other thing I have found is that the people who consider too close an affection between men and animals to be 'unnatural' are basing their prejudice on something real. It is the incompatibility of ages. It is in Lucretius. He says that centaurs cannot exist because the horse part would die before the man part. All I can do now is to remember her dead as I buried her, the cold grey jowl in the basket, and not as my heart's blood, which she was for the last eight years of our twelve. I shall never be more than half a centaur now.

I must thank you very, very much for your two letters, which have left me as amazed at your wisdom as I always was at your kindness and information. I have done what you said I was to do, or at any rate I have bought a puppy bitch. Brownie had taught me so much about setters that it seemed silly to waste the education, so I stuck to them. No setter could ever remind me of her, any more than one woman would remind you of another, except in general terms. The new arrangement looks like the fetus of a rat, but she has a pedigree rather longer than the Emperor of Japan's. She is called Cill Dara Something-or-other of Palmerston, but prefers to be called Killie, for lucidity. She nibbles for fleas in my whiskers. We are to accept the plaudits of the people of Erin next St. Patrick's day at the Kennel Club Shew, where we intend to win the Puppy Class and the Novices: in the Autumn we go to watch the Field Trials, which we win the year after. When we have collected 15 points or green stars and can call ourselves CH. in the stud book we are coming to repeat the process in England. We are to have about 4 litters of puppies. Then it is to be America: the camera men & reporters, the drive up Broadway with typists showering us with tape, the reception at the White House, the spotlights at Hollywood. In short, we are determined to make good.

If you really want a Pointer and were not suggesting him in order to encourage me, I will gladly train one for you. . . .

Do you think it would be wrong of me to write a book about Brownie, or that I ought to wait seven years before starting? I have a strong feeling that I want to write it now. . . .

I have joined the Kennel Club as a life member, as I am going to have hundreds and hundreds of setters from now on, to prevent loving one of them too much. When I went to their office about half a dozen dog-like women attended to me so faithfully and gently, and one of them was so exactly like a bull-dog, that I celebrated my entry by crying all over my check book. She was solid gold and stood by and gave moral support without speaking. I can't remember whether she barked a bit.

love from TIM

If You Can. . .

If you can start the day without caffeine or pep pills, If you can be cheerful, ignoring aches and pains, If you can resist complaining and boring people with your troubles, If you can eat the same food every day and be grateful for it, If you can understand when loved ones are too busy to give you time, If you can take criticism and blame without resentment, If you can face the world without lies and deceit, If you can relax without liquor, If you can sleep without the aid of drugs, If you can find great happiness in the simplest things in life, If you can forgive any action in the blink of an eye,

...then, you are almost as good as your dog.

Dog Sports

Entertainment for Extreme Canine Athletes and Their Humans

Here are a few ways dogs can compete or just chill out. Dog sports not only provide an outlet for high-strung pets, but they are also a great way for humans to socialize. Many an alliance has formed over a fine weimaraner on a sunny day.

FRISBEE experts say you should know how to throw a Frisbee before you teach your dog. Start by using multiple discs to train her to retrieve and drop, keeping your dog on a 30-foot leash. Begin with an underhanded spin that travels close to the ground. Each time she catches and drops a disc, reward her by throwing the next one. For help, try the Frisbee Dog Page, www.dogpatch.org/dogs/frisbee.cfm.

FLYBALL RACING started in the 1970s with the advent of the tennis-ball launcher. Two relay teams of four animals each race side-by-side over a 51-foot-long course comprising four jumps. Each member runs the course, triggers a ball launcher, retrieves the ball, returns over the jumps, and releases the next dog. The first team to have all four dogs finish without error wins. Look for the North American Flyball Assoc. at (nafadb.flyball.org/public.shtml).

DOCK DIVING, a "big air" event patterned after the long jump, involves racing down a dock and jumping as far off the end into the water as possible. Check out www.dockdogs.com for information about big-air dogs and their competitions.

TERRIER RACES and steeplechases are the favorites of little tykes. Learn about these events and see photos of pint-size doggy dragsters and hurdlers at www.workingterrier.com.

Dog Dietetics 101

The Association of American Feed Control Officials {AAFCO} regulates the labeling of pet food. Feeding directions specify the amount of food recommended based on weight. These are helpful as a starting point, but nutritional needs vary by breed, metabolism, and activity level. Talk to your vet!

Most owners feed some, if not all, of their dogs' intake in the form of dry food.

ADULT DOGS usually get two meals per day, depending on your vet's recommendation—OR you can ration out all food as treats for good behavior.

PUPPIES should be fed as many times as they defecate per day (between three and six)—OR, as above, ration out all food as treats for desirable behavior, *especially* when housebreaking and chew-training. Rationing out food as rewards is preferable.

VETS AND TRAINERS AGREE Do not "free feed." A constant food source sitting there can lead to undereating or overeating.

LEADER OF THE PACK Don't feed your dog just before you eat. Since you are "top dog" in your house, it will make sense to your dog that you eat before he does. Also, don't encourage begging by feeding at the table. Consider training your dog to hold a well-mannered sit, a behavior that is incompatible with begging, at a distance from diners.

How Much is Too Much?

Dogs get fat from too much grub and too little exercise. A dog can become obese in a few years by eating 10 percent more than he needs. If Fido gets a high-calorie biscuit, decrease his meal ration.

FEEL THE BURN Design a workout schedule that includes your dog. Not enough time to work out? Train him! Then you can take him with you on errands or even to work.

LOVE HANDLES Regardless of build, your dog is overweight if you can't feel her ribs. ***Do not attempt a weight-loss program*** without the help of a nutritional expert. You could feed your dog too little calcium, among other things, and not realize it.

What Not to Feed

Some foods for human consumption are toxic to canines; specifically grapes, raisins, salt, processed sugar, chocolate, and onions and garlic. Ingesting **CHOCOLATE** requires immediate treatment; its theobromide can kill. **ONIONS** and **GARLIC** contain the toxin thiosulphite, which causes possibly fatal hemolytic anemia (garlic less so). **CORN** can be less digestible for dogs, so when baking pet treats, use oat, rice, or wheat flour. Turkey, pork, and soy are on the list of suspects when dogs have gastrointestinal problems, as these foods are not as digestible as chicken.

New Year's Resolutions for Dogs

■ Have a one—night stand with a street mutt.

■ I will no longer be enslaved to the sound of the can opener.

■ Circulate petition that leg humping be a juried competition in major dog shows.

■ Call PETA and tell them what that surgical mask-wearing freak does to us when no one is around.

■ Take time from busy schedule to stop and smell the behinds.

■ Always scoot my bottom before licking it.

■ Grow opposable thumb; break into pantry; decide for MYSELF how much food is *too* much.

■ Kill the sock! Must kill the sock.

■ I will not chase the darn stick unless I see it LEAVE HIS HAND.

Canine Crackups

Confession of A Glutton

by Don Marquis

After i ate my dinner then i ate
part of a shoe
i found some archies by a bathroom pipe
and ate them too
i ate some glue
i ate a bone that had got nice and ripe
six weeks buried in the ground
i ate a little mousie that i found
i ate some sawdust from the cellar floor
it tasted sweet
i ate some outcast meat
and some roach paste by the pantry door
and then the missis had some folks to tea
nice folks who petted me

and so i ate
cakes from a plate
i ate some polish that they use
for boots and shoes
and then i went back to the missis
    swell tea party
i guess i must have eat too hearty
of something maybe cake
for then came the earthquake
you should have seen the missis face
and when the boss came in she said
no wonder that dog hangs his head
he knows hes in disgrace
i am a well intentioned little pup
but sometimes things come up
to get a little dog in bad
and now i feel so very very sad
but the boss said never mind old scout
time wears disgraces out

*S*ealing these treats with a milk glaze helps keep them fresh and crunchy, and using canola oil provides essential fatty acids. Be sure to let family members know they're for the dog!

For treats:
1 package yeast
$^1/_4$ cup lukewarm water
2 tablespoons olive or canola oil
2 cups low-sodium chicken broth
$^1/_2$ cup powdered milk
$^1/_2$ cup grated Parmesan or Romano cheese
1 teaspoon dried oregano
4 tablespoons fresh parsley, very finely chopped
$^3/_4$ to $1^1/_4$ cups whole wheat flour
$^1/_2$ cup rye flour
$^1/_2$ cup rice flour
1 cup cracked wheat

For glaze:
1 egg
2 tablespoons chicken or beef broth or 1 tablespoon milk

1. Preheat oven to 325°F.

2. In a large bowl, dissolve yeast in water. Add oil, broth, dry milk, cheese, oregano, and parsley, and mix well.

3. Gradually blend in the rest of the treat ingredients, adding enough wheat flour to form a stiff dough. Knead until smooth and shape into a ball.

4. Transfer to your rolling surface and roll to $^1/_2$-inch thickness. Cut out shapes, gathering and using leftover pieces.

5. Place on ungreased baking sheets and bake for about 20–30 minutes.

6. Whisk egg and liquid together to make the glaze.

7. Apply glaze, turn, reglaze, and bake for another 20–30 minutes.

6. Cool on a rack. Refrigerate for 1 week, or freeze indefinitely.

Makes up to 4 dozen treats

Cheesy Treats

Five Crucial Food Groups According to Dogs

1. In the bowl. **A good foundation, but important to supplement with other groups.**

2. Off the table. **Most varied group, but best eaten when no one is looking.**

3. On the floor. **A nutritious way to snack between meals.**

4. Grass — **taken at least once a day to enable vomit activity (vomit activity best engaged in while resting head on caretaker's lap).**

5. Poop. **At least once a day for overall digestive happiness. May be taken topically via rolling in it. Be sure to lick owner in face after ingestion.**

A door is what a dog is perpetually
on the wrong side of. —Ogden Nash

343

Party Manners

"Help!*" you cry. "Our dog is...well, a real dog! He jumps, he humps, he sniffs. We can dress him up but we can't let him come to our party." Here's a way to have your business associates buzzing around the water cooler about your incredibly well-mannered canine.*

Jumping, Humping, and Other Obnoxious Behaviors

DO practice the sit with your dog (p. 264) before company arrives, so that he is familiar with the behavior expected of him. Have a family member enter the room. Each time they enter, ask the dog to sit, then reward him. Your dog will associate a person entering the room with the sit, and will offer it without being cued. The second he does this, let him know how good he is! Give him a treat and yourself a pat on the back. You have trained the dog to sit instead of jumping on someone and spilling their red wine.

As company arrives, have a family member continue to reward the dog each time he sits when a guest enters. Ask guests not to call the dog or offer food. Expect mishaps at first. Be patient; it's not easy to learn to hold a sit when you are excited about new people, nor is it easy for humans to keep their hands off a cute pup! As you continue training, try to get the dog to hold the sit longer before you say "okay." Give him some time to romp with the partygoers, but the moment he starts being obnoxious, ask him to sit again, and be sure to praise him.

DON'T turn your pooch loose on the crowd and then yell at him for "bad" doggy behavior. He won't understand.

Superhero Pit Bull Terrier

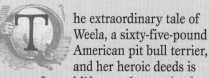

The extraordinary tale of Weela, a sixty-five-pound American pit bull terrier, and her heroic deeds is one of a real-life superhero animal. On the domestic stage, Weela played the ultimate protector. While watching Gary, her 11-year-old son, playing in the backyard, Lori Watkins was shocked to see Weela lunge at the child, sending the boy soaring. But then she saw what provoked Weela—a large rattlesnake was sinking its fangs into the dog's face. The terrier had shielded the child with her own body from the deadly bite of the snake—and afterward made a total recovery from the attack! On a larger stage, Weela played the protector of both man and beast during a watery siege in Southern California. In January 1993, following heavy rains, the Tijuana River burst from its dam, sending a torrent of disaster down its normally sedate route. During the following month, Weela led rescue teams to horses stranded on a manure pile and surrounded by floodwaters, battled heavy rains for 6 hours to deliver food to stranded and starving dogs and one cat, and guided people who were attempting to move from a raging section of the river to shallower crossings. Weela saved a total of more than 70 living creatures. 🐾

Obituary

by E. B. White

Daisy ("Black Watch Debatable") died December 22, 1931, when she was hit by a Yellow Cab in University Place. At the moment of her death she was smelling the front of a florist's shop. It was a wet day, and the cab skidded up over the curb—just the sort of excitement that would have amused her, had she been at a safer distance. She is survived by her mother, Jeannie; a brother, Abner; her father, whom she never knew; and two sisters, whom she never liked. She was three years old.

Daisy was born at 65 West Eleventh Street in a clothes closet at two o'clock of a December morning in 1928. She came, as did her sisters and brothers, as an unqualified surprise to her mother, who had for several days previously looked with a low-grade suspicion on the box of bedding that had been set out for the delivery, and who had gone into the clothes closet merely because she had felt funny and wanted a dark, awkward place to feel funny in. Daisy was the smallest of the litter of seven, and the oddest.

Her life was full of incident but not of accomplishment. Persons who knew her only slightly regarded her as an opinionated little bitch, and said so; but she had a small circle of friends who saw through her, cost what it did. At Speyer Hospital, where she used to go when she was indisposed, she was known as "Whitey," because, the man told me, she was black. All her life she was subject to moods, and her feeling about horses laid her sanity open to question. Once she slipped her leash and chased a horse for three blocks through heavy traffic, in the carking belief that she was an effective agent against horses. Drivers of teams, seeing her only in the moments of her delirium, invariably leaned far out of their seats and gave tongue, mocking her; and thus made themselves even more ridiculous, for the moment, than Daisy.

She had a stoical nature, and spent the latter part of her life an invalid, owing to an injury to her right hind leg. Like many invalids, she developed a rather objectionable cheerfulness, as though to deny that she had cause for rancor. She also developed, without instruction or encouragement, a curious habit of holding people firmly by the ankle without actually biting them—a habit that gave her an immense personal advantage and won her many enemies. As far as I know, she never even broke the thread of a sock, so delicate was her grasp (like a retriever's), but her point of view was questionable, and her attitude was beyond explaining to the person whose ankle was at stake. For my own amusement, I often tried to diagnose this quirkish temper, and I think I understand it: she suffered form a chronic perplexity, and it relieved her to take hold of something.

She was arrested once, by Patrolman Porko. She enjoyed practically everything in life except motoring, an exigency to which she submitted silently, without joy, and without nausea. She never took pains to discover, conclusively, the things that might have diminished her curiosity and spoiled her taste. She died sniffing life, and enjoying it. 🐾

349

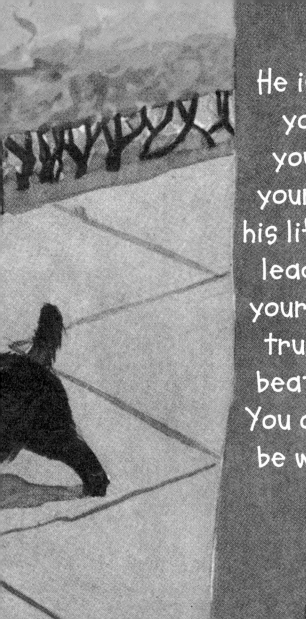

He is your friend, your partner, your defender, your dog. You are his life, his love, his leader. He will be yours, faithful and true, to the last beat of his heart. You owe it to him to be worthy of such devotion.

—Anonymous

Acknowledgments

"Dogs Vis-à-vis Cats" by Roy Blount, Jr. Reprinted by permission of International Creative Management, Inc. Copyright © 1988 by Roy Blount, Jr.

"Fred, A Dog Gone but not Forgotten" copyright © 1984 by Thomas M. Boyd. Originally published in *The Wall Street Journal*.

"The Dollar Dog," from *Doodle Soup* by John Ciardi. Copyright © 1985 by Myra J. Ciardi. Reprinted by permission of Houghton Mifflin Company. All rights reserved.

"Another Reason Why I Don't Keep a Gun in the House" from *The Apple That Astonished Paris*, reprinted by permission of University of Arkansas Press. Copyright © 1989 by Billy Collins.

"#86" from *A Far Rockaway of the Heart*, copyright © 1997 by Lawrence Ferlinghetti. Reprinted by permission of New Directions Publishing Corp.

"Let's Hit the Road" from *Good Dog*, poems by Maya Gottfried, text © Maya Gottfried.

"Roy" from *James Herriot's Dog Stories* by James Herriot. Copyright © 1986 by the author and reprinted by permission of St. Martin's Press.

"Poor Rover" from *The Collected Poems of Langston Hughes* by Langston Hughes, copyright © 1994 by The Estate of Langston Hughes. Used by permission of Alfred A. Knopf, a division of Random House, Inc.

"A Woman's Best Friend" by Erica Jong. Copyright ©2001 Erica Mann Jong, All rights reserved. Used by permission of the author.

"The Color of Joy" from *Pack of Two* by Caroline Knapp, copyright © 1998 by Caroline Knapp. Used by permission of The Dial Press/Dell Publishing, a division of Random House, Inc.

Excerpt from *Lassie Come Home* by Eric Knight. First published as a short story in the *Saturday Evening Post*. Copyright © 1938 by the Curtis Publishing Company. Copyright renewed 1966 by Jere Knight, Betty Noyes Knight, Winifred Knight Mewborn, and Jennie Knight Moore. Reprinted by permission of the Knight Management Trust.

"A Conversation with My Dogs" by Merrill Markoe from *What My Dogs Have Taught Me*. Copyright © 1992 by Merrill Markoe. Reprinted with the permission of Random House, Inc.

"Confessions of a Glutton" from *The Lives and Times of Archy and Mehitabel* by Don Marquis, copyright © 1927, 1930, 1933, 1935, 1950 by Doubleday, a division of Random house, Inc. Used by permission of Doubleday, a division of Random House, Inc.

Excerpt from *A Dog's Life* by Peter Mayle, copyright © 1995 by Escargot Productions, Ltd. Used by permission of Alfred A. Knopf, a division of Random House, Inc.

Excerpt from "Stickeen" from *An Adventure with a Dog and a Glacier* by John Muir (Boston: Houghton Mifflin, 1909).

"To a Foolish Dog" copyright © 1972 by Ogden Nash. Reprinted by permission of Curtis Brown, Ltd.

"Ode to the Dog" from *Odes to Common Things* by Pablo Neruda. Copyright © 1994 by Pablo Neruda and Fundacion Pablo Neruda (Odes in Spanish); Copyright © 1994 by Ken Krabbenhoft (Odes in English); Copyright © 1994 by Ferris Cook (Illustrations and Compilation). By permission of Little, Brown and Co., Inc.

"Verse for a Certain Dog" from *The Portable Dorothy Parker* by Dorothy Parker, edited by Brendan Gill, copyright © 1928, renewed © 1956 by Dorothy Parker. Used by permission of Viking Penguin, a division of Penguin Group (USA) Inc.

The Soul of a Dog from "Fish Whistle" by Daniel Pinkwater. Reprinted by permission of Da Capo Press, a member of Perseus Books, LLC.

Excerpt from "Sleeping with the Pack" by Michael J. Rosen, copyright © 2003 by Michael J. Rosen. Used by permission of Michael J. Rosen.

From *Travels with Charley* by John Steinbeck, copyright © 1961, 1962 by the Curtis Publishing Co., © 1962 by John Steinbeck, renewed © 1990 by Elaine Steinbeck, Thom Steinbeck, and John Steinbeck IV. Used by permission of Viking Penguin, a division of Penguin Group (USA) Inc.

"But Mom Didn't Like Dogs" reprinted by permission of Dr. Donald R. Stoltz.

"The Thin Red Leash" by James Thurber, copyright © 1955 by James Thurber. Copyright © renewed 1983 by Helen Thurber and Rosemary A. Thurber. Reprinted by arrangement with Rosemary A. Thurber and the Barbara Hogenson Agency.

"Crimes Against Dog" reprinted by permission of The Wendy Weil Agency, Inc. First published by Crown in *Dog is My Co-Pilot*. © 2003 by Alice Walker.

E. B. White to the ASPCA from "Two Letters, Both Open" from *The Second Tree from the Corner* by E.B. White. Copyright © 1951 by E. B. White. Reprinted by permission of HarperCollins Publishers.

"Obituary" copyright © by E.B. White. Copyright © renewed 1959 by E.B. White. Originally appeared in *The New Yorker*. Reprinted by permission of HarperCollins Publishers.

Illustrations

Jacket & case: McClelland Barclay; pg. 4-7: C. Ambler; pg. 8: Zito; pg. 12: R. Rogers; pg. 21: Albert Staehle; pg. 27: Chenet; pg. 49: Wall; pg. 52: H. Fihlemo; pg. 53: Clara Unqell; pg. 63, 130-131, 233, 286: Bufford; pg. 73, 306-307, 343; pg. 85, 89, 93: Charles Livingston Bull; pg. 95, 249: A. Cucchi; pg. 99: Gene Klebe; pg. 100, 143, 175: B. Butler; pg. 105: F. Quidenur; pg. 108: Hy Hintermeisterr; pg. 109: Maurice Day; pg. 110: Beinlundtwail; pg. 117: T. Aueline; pg. 124, 125: E. Dorothy Rees; pg. 137: Ulail; pg. 139: Ellen H. Clapsaddle; pg. 146: Tadé Styka; pg. 155: John Gee; pg 159: F. Barrey; pg. 185: C. M. Burd; pg. 197: Freixas; pg. 205: GHT; pg. 218, 221, 224, 226: Diana Thorne; pg. 73, 228, 229, 306, 307, 343: Benjamin Rabier; pg. 231: Helena Maguire; pg. 246: A. Vimaz; pg. 249: A. Cucchi; pg. 252: C. Coles Phillips; pg. 261: D. Gobbis; pg. 272: Edwin Megargee; pg. 277: J. Rivst; pg. 292, 293: Hy Seidler; pg. 295: Emmett Watson; pg. 298: Dorothy Dixon; pg. 305: Norman Rockwell; pg. 310, 333, 341: Alfred Mainzer; pg. 315: Woolley; pg. 322: H.V. Preen; pg. 327: Maude West Watson; pg. 335: G.S. Studdy; pg. 345: Frank Hart; pg. 350-351: Marion Moran Cook